Contents

Setting Up Your Room

- Are you sitting in the center of a bare-walled room with desks stacked in one corner and boxes of supplies stacked in another?

- Are you looking for a new idea to spark your creativity?

- Are you tired of the room arrangement in your classroom?

This section provides ideas on how to begin the overwhelming task of preparing your classroom and yourself for the year ahead.

Contents

First, take some time to think about your priorities. Focus on one priority at a time. Decide what your classroom is all about.

What is your instructional focus?

- Will I emphasize reading and books?

  If so, your classroom library and reading area will become the key part of your classroom.

- Is hands-on science my special focus?

  You will need to provide a science supply area as well as working space.

- What technology will be a part of my everyday routine?

  If your use of technology includes a computer center, consider electrical outlets and wiring as you develop your floor plan.

Where will instruction take place?

- Where will students be for most direct instruction? At their desks? On the floor? In small groups?

  If your students will be on the floor for instruction, arrange your room so that a large open space is available.

- Will classroom centers be a part of the instructional plan?

- Will my students keep logbooks or portfolios?

  If so, plan an accessible storage space for them.

Will there be other adults in the classroom?

- Are parents often included in classroom activities?

  If so, provide a spot for their coats and belongings, a board for quick instructions or information, and an area for them to work with individual students.

- Will you have a student teacher? Intern? Instructional aide?

  Provide a place for their belongings. They need to feel at home. This is their classroom too.

What is the theme of the upcoming year?

- What is the school theme for the year?
- Is there a grade-level theme?
- Do I want to have a classroom theme?
- How will my classroom reflect these themes?

Helpful Hint

As you select themes, be sure to include them on your bulletin boards and in communications with parents.

4

What To Do First

Make your classroom inviting and workable.

- Analyze your room.

- Define areas for specific activities.

- Consider traffic patterns. Leave space for your students and you to move about easily.

- Ensure easy access to instructional centers.

- Make sure that all students have a clear view of teaching areas.

Possible Seating Plans

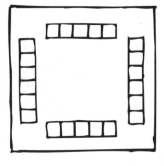 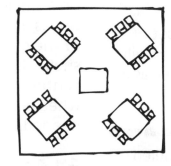 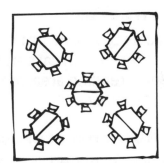

 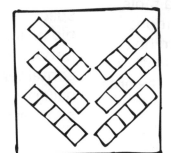 

How to Plan Your School Year • EMC 779

Create work areas in your classroom that match your instructional style and focus—a small throw rug brings a feeling of warmth and helps to define the space intended for an activity. Shelves, crates, desks, and tables can act as dividers to establish work areas.

Choose the work areas you will include in your planning.

Independent Reading Area

Bookshelves, lawn chairs, pillows, and baskets of books create an inviting spot for independent reading.

Reading and Listening Area

A recliner, a small table, a large rug, and a bookshelf create a great area for reading aloud.

Reader's Theater

Add a few pillows to a platform or set of porch steps covered with carpet. You will have a multilevel reading area, as well as a stage for performances.

Science Work and Storage Area

Organize science lab materials in labeled tubs with lids. Slip the tubs under a table. Add an easel for recording observations. Use divided trays on the tabletop to hold supplies used in the current investigation. The trays will help students tidy up the area.

A Writing Area

Hanging panels list the different steps in the writing process and define this area reserved for eager writers. Include a director's chair for authors who choose to share their work.

A Cooking Center with Built-in Storage

If cooking is part of your curriculum, you may want to designate one shelf as your kitchen. Make sure that the shelf is near a sink or water tub and includes access to an electrical outlet.

A Research Station

Encourage research with a designated station. Include print resources—an encyclopedia, an atlas, a dictionary, and collections of appropriate nonfiction books, as well as electronic resources—CD-ROMs, electronic encyclopedias, and an Internet connection.

A Listening Center on Wheels

Short on room? Consider a listening center on a small cart. Put the tape recorder and books, papers, and pencils on the top shelf of the cart. Hang headsets on the second shelf. Pile pillows on the bottom shelf. This center may be shared by a grade level and wheeled from classroom to classroom as needed.

An Art Gallery

Space for displaying student art can be a big problem. Suspend narrow clothesline between two ladders or easels. Hang a container of clothespins on one rung. Your gallery can double as a drying place. Hang pictures back to back to increase space.

Writing Area

Science Area

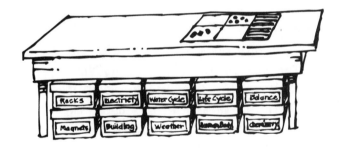

Books

Art Gallery

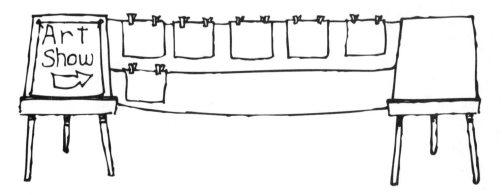

How to Plan Your School Year • EMC 779

Successful organization depends on your ability to find information and materials when your students need them. You will not be the only individual putting things away, so it is important to designate a place for things that are used frequently. Label storage areas so that students and visitors can see where things belong.

Seasonal and Curricular Materials

Take the time to sort and organize materials into boxes. Label the boxes clearly. Group the boxes by season or curricular area for storage.

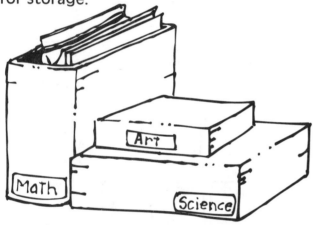

Ask your local school supply store or discount center to save the boxes that paper portfolios come in. Cover the boxes with contact paper and use them.

Creating Storage Space

Create storage areas with inexpensive shelves and tubs or crates. The crates can be put on bookshelves to create easily accessible reading and writing files or portfolio storage areas.

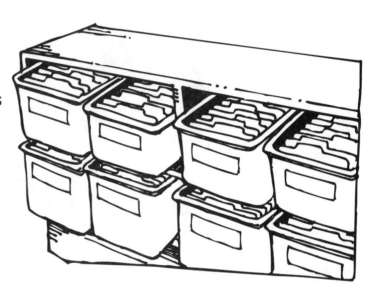

A Supply Table

A centralized supply table can hold the things needed for the day's work. Wire baskets, tubs, and crates will keep your supplies organized. Students should be responsible for picking up and returning the materials that they need.

Found Storage Space

Check your room for unused space. The top of the coat rack, underneath a table, and the sides of a room divider can become a storage resource.

Unusual Containers

Hang a shoe bag. Use it to hold paperback books or center supplies.

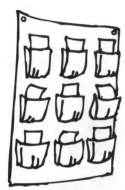

Baskets serve as attractive organizers. Fill a basket with your attendance supplies. Put the basket in a convenient spot. Fill another basket with work supplies for a small group—pencils, scissors, crayons, glue sticks, and paper. Keep the basket next to the work area. Use baskets creatively!

First-Aid Kit

If your school nurse doesn't provide a classroom first-aid kit, prepare your own. A lunch box makes a great container. Include bandages, liquid soap, first-aid cream, disposable rubber gloves, cotton balls, and petroleum jelly. Teach universal precautions and explain the use of each of the supplies to students. Then encourage them, with your approval, to care for their own minor injuries.

Lunch Tub

Use a large tub or laundry basket as a lunch tub. Label the tub with your name and room number. Add a distinctive picture for early primary classrooms. Have students put their lunches from home in the tub as they come into the classroom. At lunchtime, students can pick up their lunches on the way to the eating area. A student helper can carry the empty tub to the eating area so that, after eating, lunch boxes can be put back in the tub before students go outside for recess.

Pencil Bank

Keep a container of sharpened pencils and an identical empty container labeled "Dull" on a tray in an easily accessible area. Whenever a student needs a sharp pencil, he or she will put the dull pencil into the container labeled "Dull" and take a sharp pencil. This procedure eliminates the noise of the pencil sharpener. At the end of the day, a helper can sharpen all the dull pencils and transfer them to the container of sharpened pencils.

The single, most helpful organizational space in your classroom may be your student work folders or cubbies. Each student will have a place to put finished work, as well as notes to go home.

Folders can be simple or more complex. You might choose to use one or more of the following:

- a folder in the student's desk
- a hanging folder system in a central location
- labeled shelf cubbies
- cardboard pockets mounted on a board or against a wall

Some Convenient Cubbies

Cardboard pockets can be posted in a group on a room divider or hung in a single row from a board with sawhorse legs. The pockets can be reused year after year. Decorate each one with a name tag and a photo.

Cover cereal boxes with contact paper and stack them. Label each slot and you have a set of inexpensive cubbies.

Bolt large vegetable cans or large cardboard ice-cream cartons together to create round cubbies.

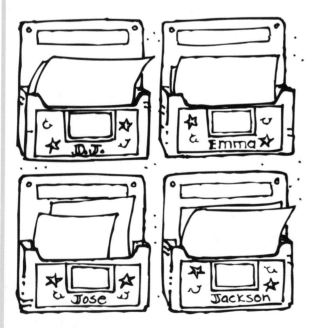

How to Plan Your School Year • EMC 779

What Will I Do with Student Work?

Take-Home Folders

To facilitate the process of taking home notes and completed work, provide a take-home folder. This folder will go home daily or on a designated day each week. It is returned to school empty with parent signatures and comments the following day.

Your take-home folder may simply be a large manila envelope, or you can create a sturdy, easy-to-carry pocket following these steps:

1. Give each student a large manila folder.

2. Students decorate the folder on the front and back.

3. Open the folders and laminate them.

4. Refold the folders and staple the sides.

5. Cover the staples with fabric tape.

6. Write student names and your room number with permanent marker.

 Helpful Hint

Tape a library card pocket to the front of the take-home folder for special messages that might be lost in the big folder.

11

Develop your own places for specific supplies. Check out these storage ideas suggested by teachers.

Rulers

Keep your rulers in a patio-edging block. Check your local garden store for unique shapes and sizes. Glue felt to the bottom of the block and put it on a shelf. It will be sturdy enough not to tip or spill and it's attractive.

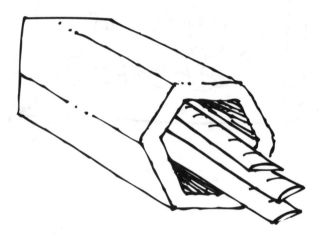

Desk Clips

Clip papers to the fronts of desks with magnetic clips. Or use clothespins and pieces of self-sticking Velcro. Attach the "fuzzy" side of the Velcro to the desks and the "toothed" side to the clothespins. You might clip corrected papers, papers to be turned in, special notes to students or parents, library cards, or student performance cards.

Scissors

Turn a small plastic storage bin upside down and stick scissors through the bottom so that the points are inside the bins.

Pencil Holders

Collect large plastic drink cups after a sporting event. Run them through the dishwasher to make sure they are clean. They will easily hold regular and colored pencils and are a big hit with sport enthusiasts. The best part? They won't cost you anything!

Room Setup Planning Sheet

Use this worksheet to focus your room setup.

Curricular Focus	**Special Factors or Student Needs**
Theme for the Year	

Draw a floor plan of your room here.

How to Plan Your School Year • EMC 779

Bulletin Boards

- Bulletin boards set the mood and tone for your classroom.

- Bulletin boards are important organizational tools.

- Bulletin boards are valuable instructional centers.

This section suggests ways to optimize your use of bulletin boards to enhance classroom learning.

Contents

Plan your bulletin boards so that you can leave the basic background and trim in place all year.

If you prefer changing backgrounds, put up several backgrounds, one on top of the other. Then when you remove the first one, there is another already in place.

File your bulletin board letters. Put all the letters for a specific caption into a single envelope or file letters alphabetically.

Cover the backs of bookshelves with cotton batting and fabric to create a floor-level bulletin board. These soft bulletin boards absorb sound.

15

What You Need

- blank calendar grid, laminated
- small finishing nails, laminated
- month labels on pages 17–27
- markers for the days, pages 29–39, laminated

What You Do

1. Buy or make a blank calendar grid.
2. Place the grid on a bulletin board.
3. Put small nails in each space. (Use a small hammer to save your fingers.)

4. Label the calendar with the current month and year. Throughout the year, change the name of the month and the year as needed.

5. Add markers for the days of the month. Decide whether you will put up one marker at a time or organize the calendar at the beginning of each month. Use the markers provided or purchase ones for each month.

January

| January | February | March | April | May | June |
| July | August | September | October | November | December |

Sunday	Monday	Tuesday	Wednesday	Thursday	Friday	Saturday
			1 Holiday	2	3	4
5	6	7	8	9	10	11
12	13	14	15 Holiday	16	17	18
19	20	21	22	23	24	25
26	27 Birthday	28	29	30	31	

16

January

January February March April May June

July August September October November December

February

January February March April May June

July August September October November December

March

January   February   March   April   May   June

July   August   September   October   November   December

April

January   February   March   April   May   June

July   August   September   October   November   December

May

January   February   March   April   May   June

July   August   September   October   November   December

June

January   February   March   April   May   June

July   August   September   October   November   December

July

January February March April May June

August September October November December

July

August

January February March April May June

August September October November December

July

September

January   February   March   April   May   June

July   August   September   October   November   December

October

January   February   March   April   May   June

July   August   September   October   November   December

November

January   February   March   April   May   June

July   August   September   October   November   December

December

January   February   March   April   May   June

July   August   September   October   November   December

○

1

○

2

○

3

○

4

○

5

○

6

○

7

○

8

○

9

○

10

○

11

○

12

13

14

15

16

17

18

19

20

21

22

23

24

25

26

27

28

29

30

31

Holiday

Birthday

Holiday

Birthday

Birthday

Make your calendar an important teaching station. Pick and choose from the activities described on pages 41–48. Establish a daily routine for completing the activities on the board.

How Many Days Have We Been in School?

A counting line helps students note number system patterns. For example, students observe that the numerals 0 through 9 repeat over and over in the ones place, while each numeral repeats ten times before changing to the next numeral in the tens place. How many times do you think the numerals repeat in the hundreds place before changing?

What You Need

- a roll of adding machine tape
- a piece of yarn or string to make a loop for hanging the roll
- a nail or hook

What You Do

1. Write a zero on the end of the tape.
2. Suspend a roll of adding machine tape on a loop of yarn at the corner of your calendar board.
3. Add a number each day. You may want to help students recognize patterns by using different colors and shapes.

   Blue—multiples of 5
   Red—circles around multiples of 10

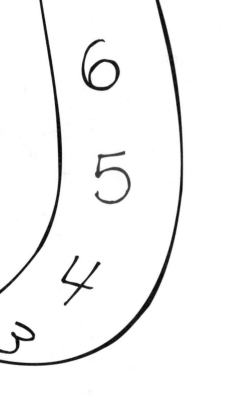

A Calendar Bank

Add a penny to the calendar bank every day. The bank balance is always organized into the fewest coins possible. This hands-on practice provides a quick daily review that helps young students remember the value of coins.

What You Need

- see-through containers (self-locking plastic bags, clear tubs, clear plastic coin purses) labeled *pennies, nickels, dimes, quarters, half-dollars, dollars*

- a "bank" (old coin purse or wallet) with five pennies, two nickels, two dimes, two quarters, two fifty-cent pieces, and a dollar bill

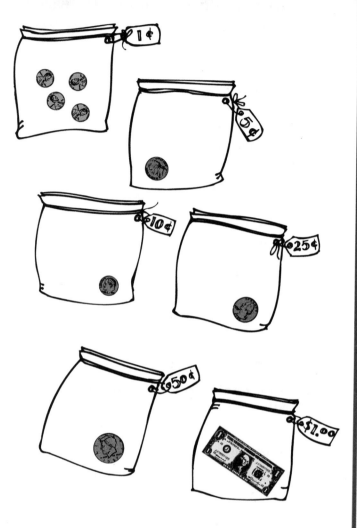

What You Do

1. Each day the banker adds one penny to the penny container.

2. The banker trades coins so that money displayed is always in the fewest possible coins.

   On the fifth day, the banker will trade five pennies for one nickel.

   On the twenty-fifth day, the banker will trade five pennies for a nickel, and then the nickel and two dimes for a quarter.

Add-a-Loop Chain

Learn to count by fives and tens with this paper chain.

What You Need

- construction paper strips in two colors (Make the loops an appropriate size for your space. 8" x 1" [20 X 2.5 cm] strips work well.)
- stapler
- paper clips or pins for fastening loops

What You Do

1. Each day add a loop to form a paper chain representing the number of days you have been in school. Use one color for four loops. Every fifth day make the loop the second color.

2. As your chain grows, fasten every tenth loop to the ceiling or bulletin board edge. Use the colored loops to practice counting by fives and tens.

Problem of the Day

Provide daily practice in math and language arts.

What You Need

- a frame for your problem
- a supply of problems

What You Do

1. Post a different problem every day.

2. Read the problem each morning.

3. Students complete the problem during the day.

4. At the end of the day, discuss student solutions and celebrate problem solving.

The local bike shop ordered 19 wheels. The shop owner wanted to make seven bicycles and/or tricycles from them. How many of each type must he make to use all of the wheels?

How to Plan Your School Year • EMC 779

Place Value Straws

This addition to your calendar board will help students understand regrouping.

What You Need

- straws
- three containers for the straws, labeled "Ones," "Tens," and "Hundreds"
- rubber bands

What You Do

1. Each day put one straw in the Ones box.

2. When the box has ten straws in it, group the straws together and fasten them with a rubber band. Move the banded bunch to the Tens box. Ten groups of ten are grouped and placed in the Hundreds box.

3. Compare the "straw number" with your daily count.

   "We've been in school 35 days.
   That's three bunches of ten straws and
   five straws in the Ones box.
   Three tens + five ones = 35."

Hundreds

Tens

Ones

Lost Tooth Graph

Collect and use data about the teeth lost by your students to provide real mathematical experiences.

What You Need

- a tooth for each month of the school year
  Reproduce the pattern on page 46.
  Mount it on construction paper.
  Write the name of each month on a different tooth.
  Laminate the teeth.

- a supply of small tooth folders—pattern on page 47

What You Do

1. Post the appropriate monthly tooth by the calendar. Whenever a student loses a tooth, write his or her name on the tooth.

2. Write a sentence about how the tooth was lost on the small tooth folder and put the tooth inside if it was lost at school.

3. Pin the tooth folder to the bulletin board or use a magnetic clip to hang it on the chalkboard until the end of the school day.

4. As an ongoing project, use the data recorded to create a graph showing the month in which the most teeth were lost.

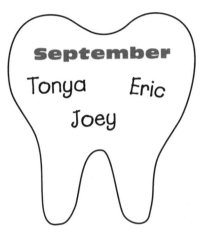

September

Tonya   Eric

Joey

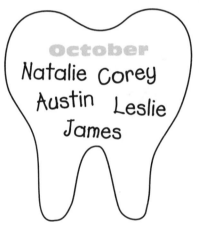

October

Natalie Corey

Austin   Leslie

James

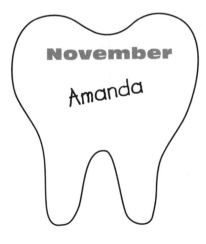

November

Amanda

	1	2	3	4	5	6	7	8	7	8
January										
February										
March										
April										
May										
June										
July										
August										
September	▓	▓	▓							
October	▓	▓	▓	▓	▓					
November	▓									
December										

Tooth Pattern

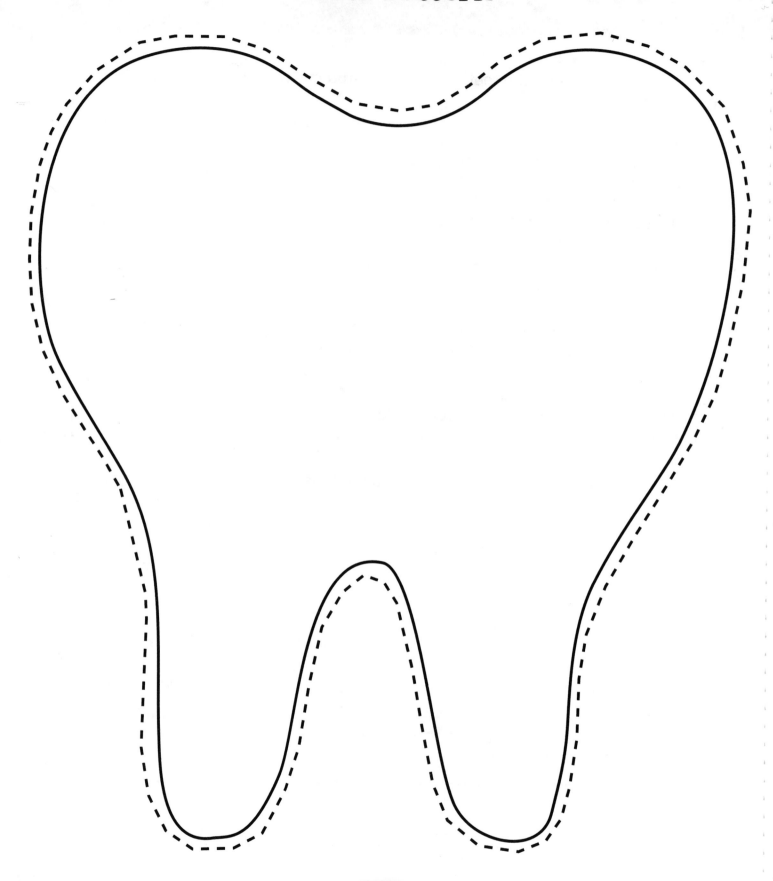

Tooth Folder Pattern

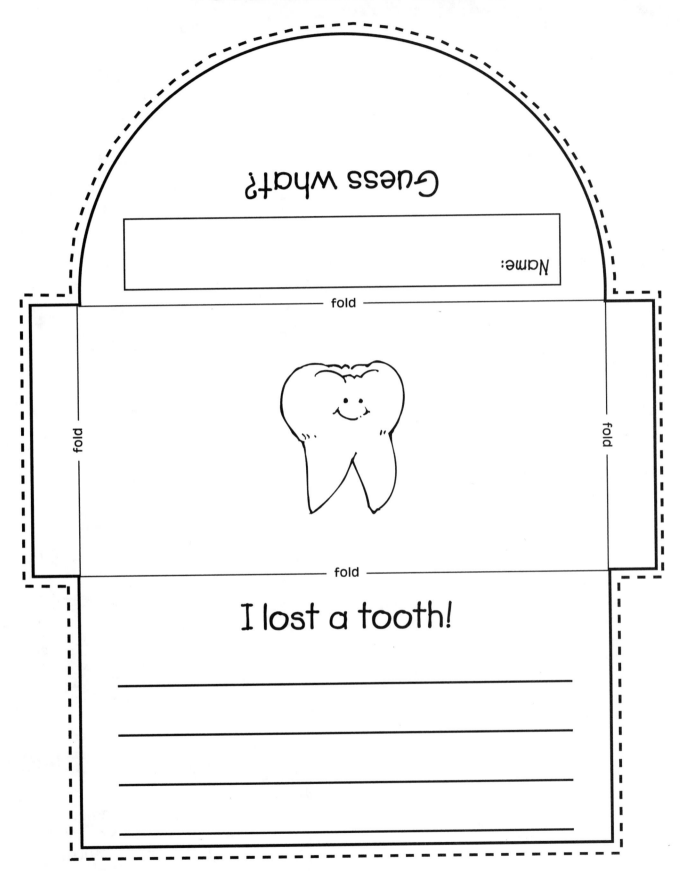

Guess what?

Name:

fold

fold

fold

fold

I lost a tooth!

Birthday Graph

Birthdays provide real data for your students to graph and analyze.

What You Need

- monthly cakes on pages 49–53
- candles on page 55, one for each student

What You Do

1. Each month post the cake for that month near the calendar board.

2. Label a candle for each student having a birthday that month.

3. At the end of each month, transfer the candles to an ongoing birthday graph.

4. Reference the graph often.

   - Use the information on the class birthday graph to make new graphs.

   - Students read the existing graph and prepare a new graph showing how many students were born on the first day of the month, the second day of the month, etc.

   - Students read the existing graph and analyze the information, preparing a new graph that shows how many girls and boys were born in each month.

Helpful Hint

Instead of cakes and candles, use gift boxes and gift tags or calendar pages with students' pictures.

Note: Use these cakes with the activity on page 48.

Birthday Cake Patterns

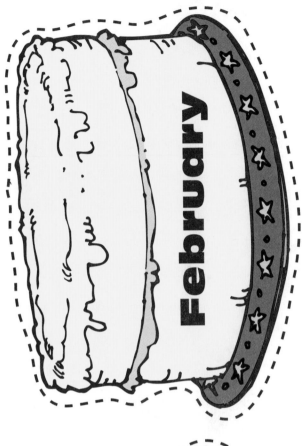

How to Plan Your School Year • EMC 779

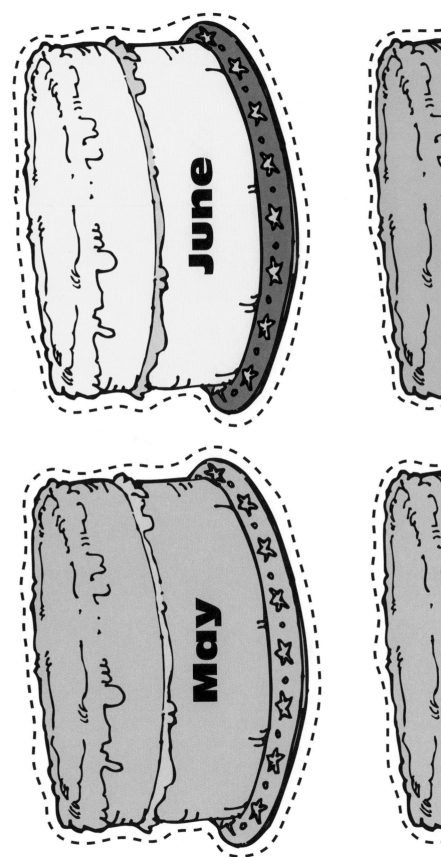

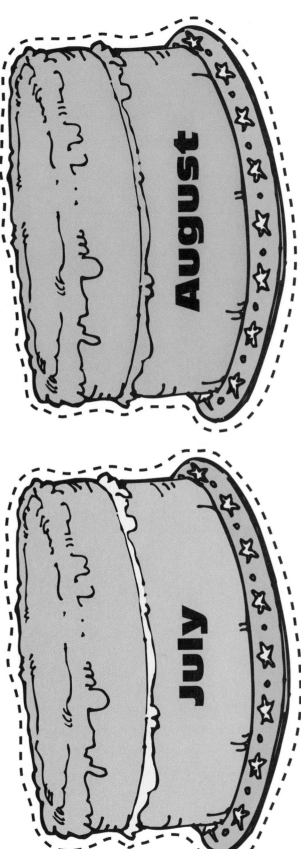

How to Plan Your School Year • EMC 779

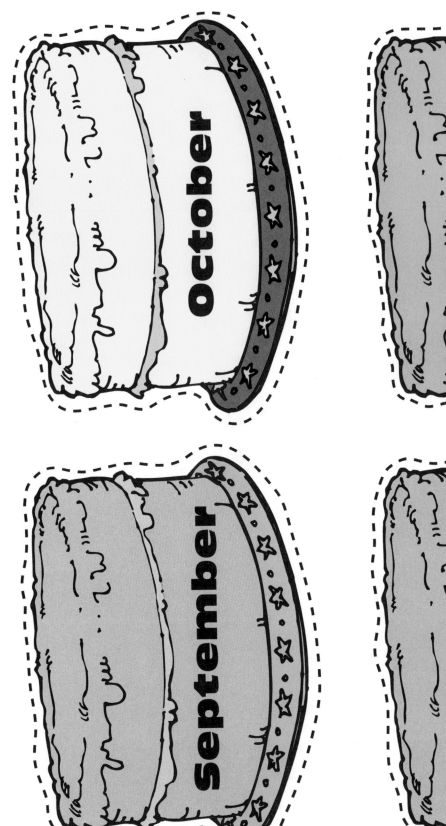

How to Plan Your School Year • EMC 779

Birthday Cake Candles

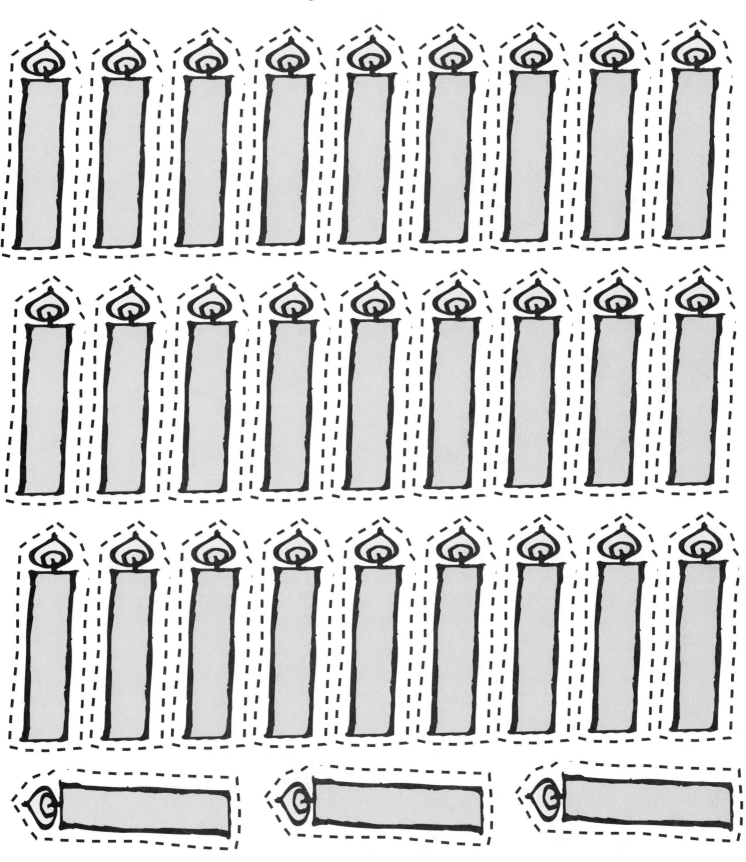

How to Plan Your School Year • EMC 779

A List of Jobs

Here are some jobs to consider for your classroom. Your list may change as you move through the year.

Helper	Possible Duties
Attendance Monitor	• carries attendance to office once it's been taken by the teacher • takes attendance
Calendar Cop	• manipulates the calendar board • reminds class of timely events
Chairperson	• stacks chairs at the end of the day • moves chairs into position
Line Leaders	• lead the lines as students move from place to place • monitor line behavior
Clean-Up Supervisor	• monitors end-of-the-day cleanup • lets class know when cleanup is necessary
Messenger	• delivers messages to others in school
Paper Passers	• help distribute papers
Librarian	• maintains the classroom library • files new books
Pencil Sharpener	• sharpens pencils in the class pencil bank at the end of the day
Lunch Box Helper	• carries a container for lunch boxes to the lunchroom and retrieves it with the empty lunch boxes following lunch
Door Holder	• holds the door when the class is going in or out
Zoo Keeper	• feeds and gives water to the classroom pets
Gardener	• waters plants in the classroom
Substitute	• fills in for absent helpers
Flag Monitor	• leads the Pledge of Allegiance • raises the flag daily
Homework Captain	• collects homework • records assignments for absent students
Equipment Monitor	• takes playground equipment to and from the playground
Center Maintenance	• straightens centers and reports needed supplies
Art Supply Monitor	• fills glue and paint as needed • organizes scrap box
Recycling Captain	• delivers classroom recyclables to school tubs
Greeter	• greets and orientates class visitors
Tech Support	• keeps computer area organized

 Helpful Hint

Establish a procedure for changing your helper board when the helpers change.

- Keep the process for changing helpers simple.
- Decide whether the change will be made daily or weekly.
- Rotate helpers in a pattern.

Classroom Jobs Charts

This page and page 59 suggest seven interesting ways to dislay your job list.

Job Wheel

Jobs are written around the spokes of a wheel. Clothespins labeled with students' names are moved around the outside of the wheel as jobs change.

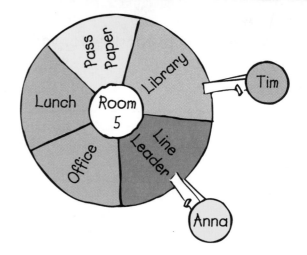

Helper Pockets

Jobs are written on pockets or small gift bags. Strips with students' names and/or photos are placed in the bags to show who has the job.

Busy Bees

Jobs are written on small hives. Bees with students' names move to a flower showing who is responsible for a certain job. (Use cutouts on pages 61–71 to make this chart.)

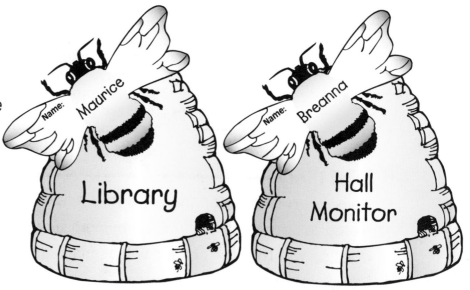

Puzzle

Jobs are written on puzzle pieces. Labeled photos are attached to the puzzle pieces to indicate who has each job.

Stars

Jobs are written on stars. Space shuttles with students' names fly to the stars for job assignments. (Use cutouts on pages 73–85 to make this chart.)

Garden of Helpers

Jobs are written on leaves. Duties of a specific job may be listed on another leaf. Students' photos and names are posted in the center of the flower. (Use patterns on page 87 to make this chart)

Clothesline

Jobs are written on shirts. Pockets with students' names are attached to shirts to show who has each job. (Use patterns on page 60 to make this chart.)

59

Shirt and Pocket Patterns

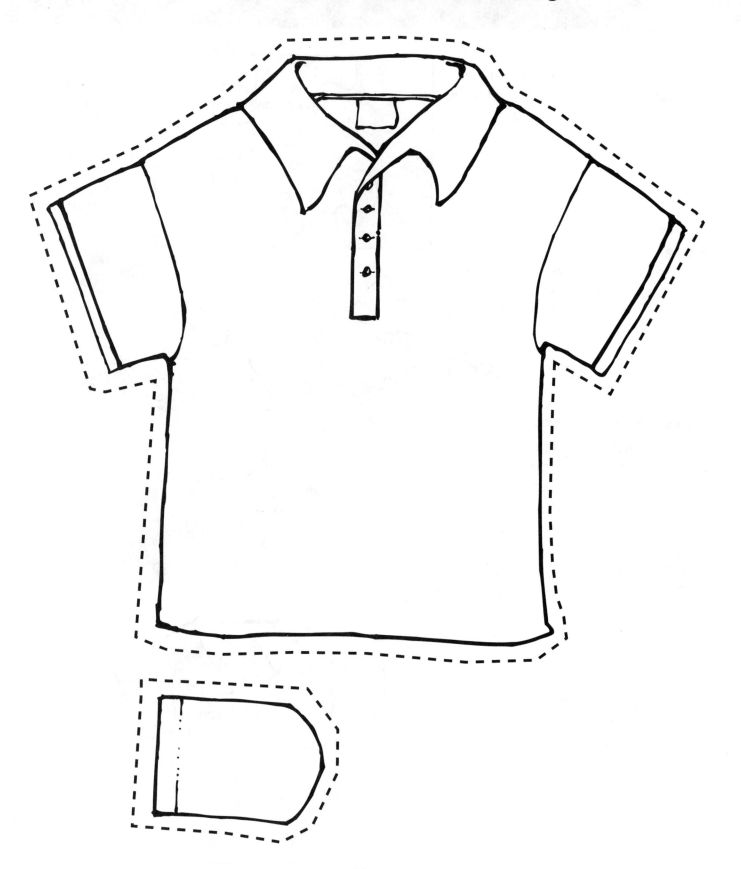

How to Plan Your School Year • EMC 779

Note: Use with the Busy Bees Job Chart on page 58. Label the hives with classroom jobs.

Hive Cutouts

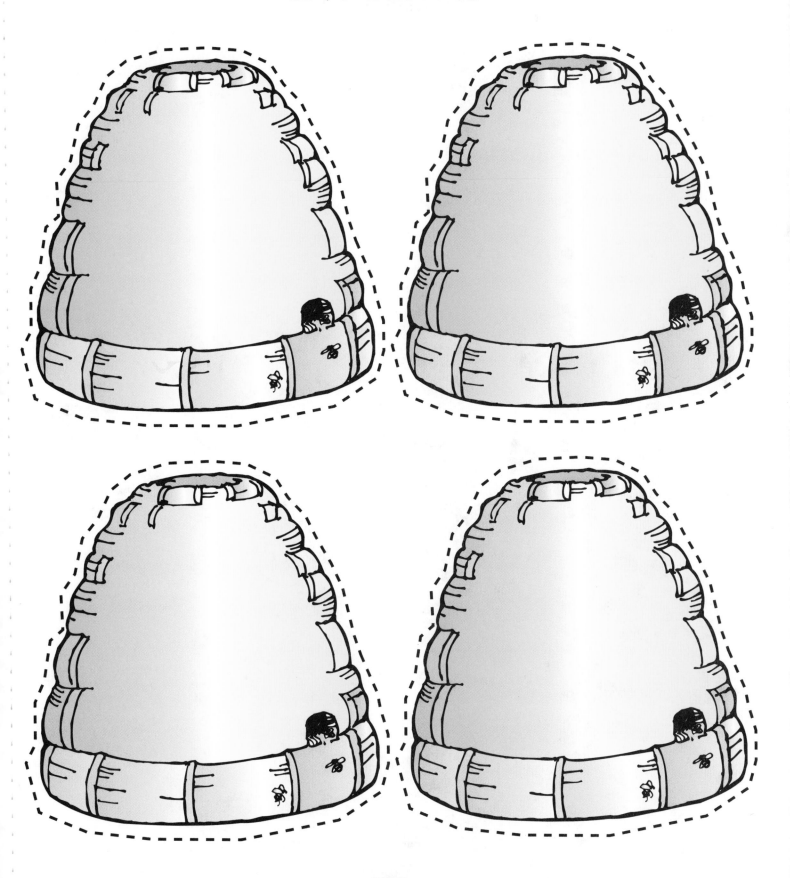

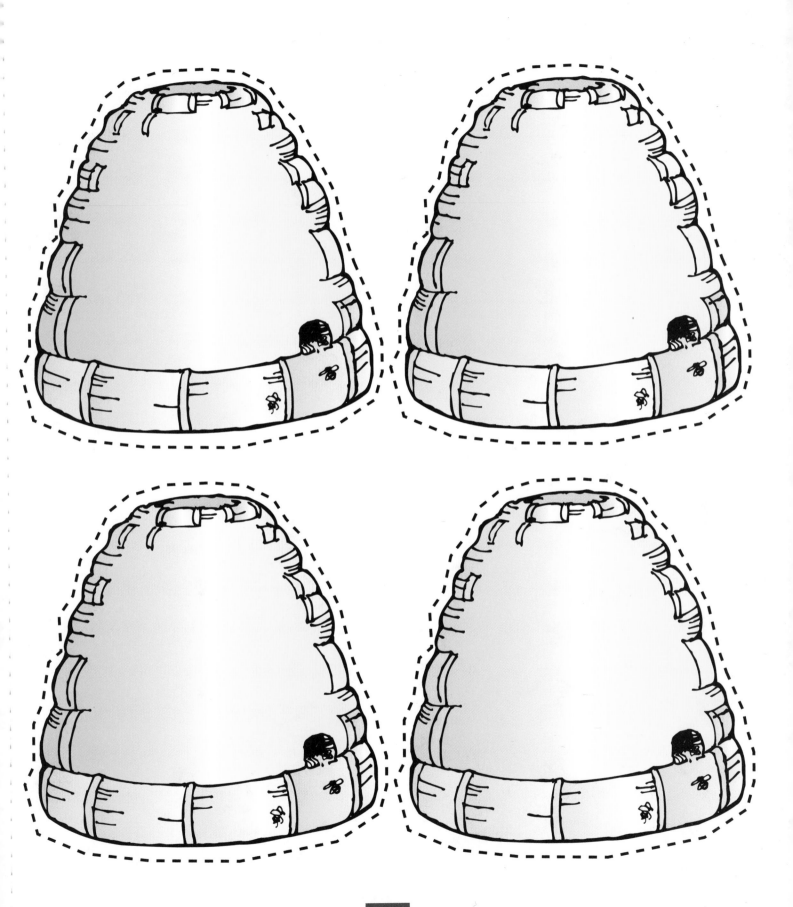

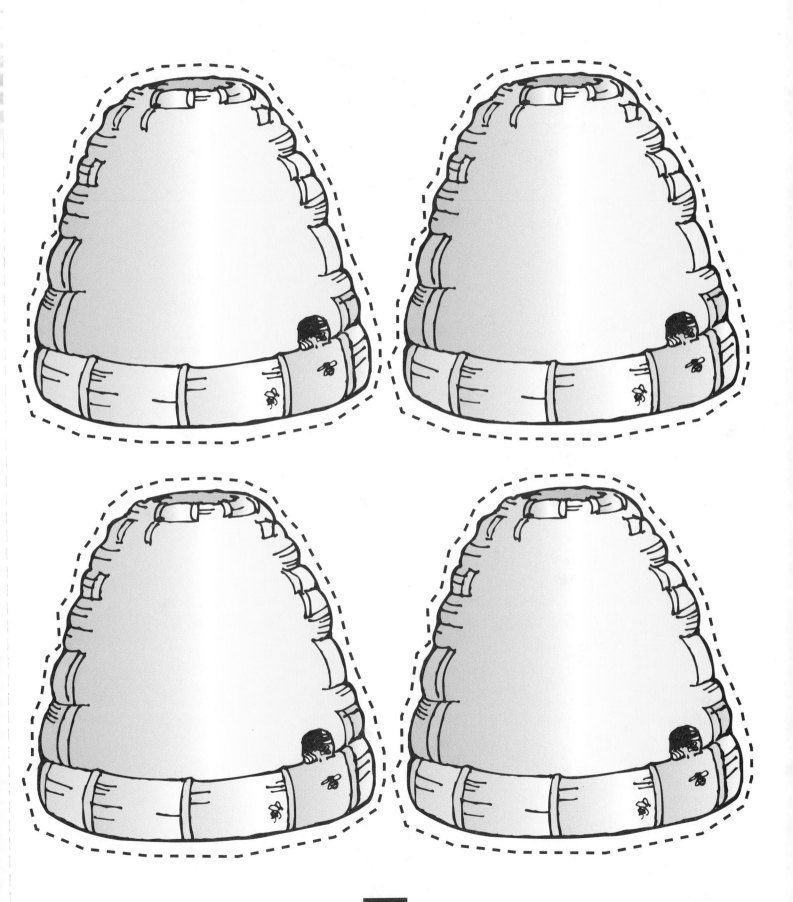

Busy Bee Cutouts

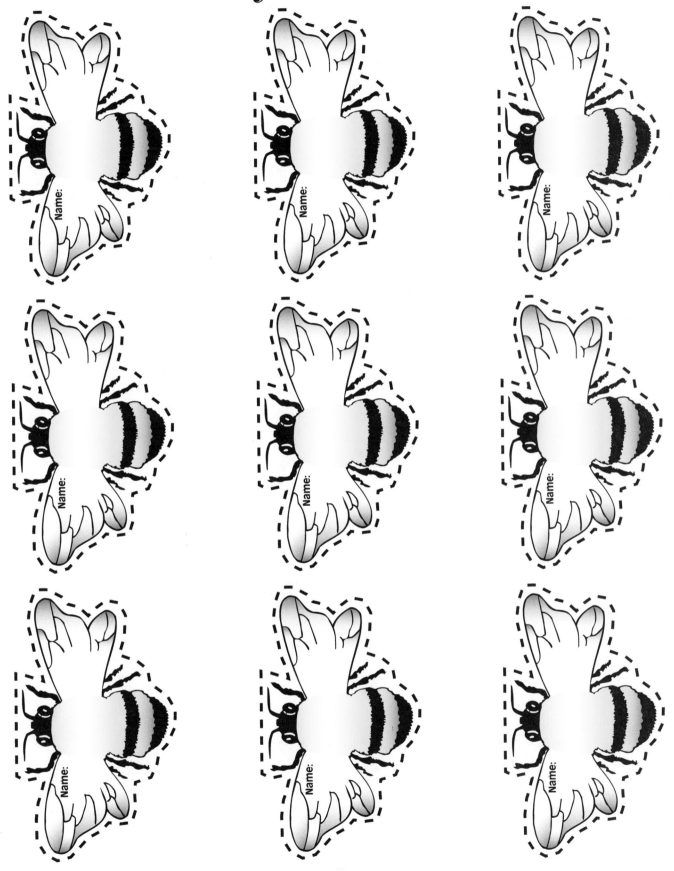

How to Plan Your School Year • EMC 779

Note: Use with the Busy Bees Job Chart on page 58. Label one bee for each student in your classroom.

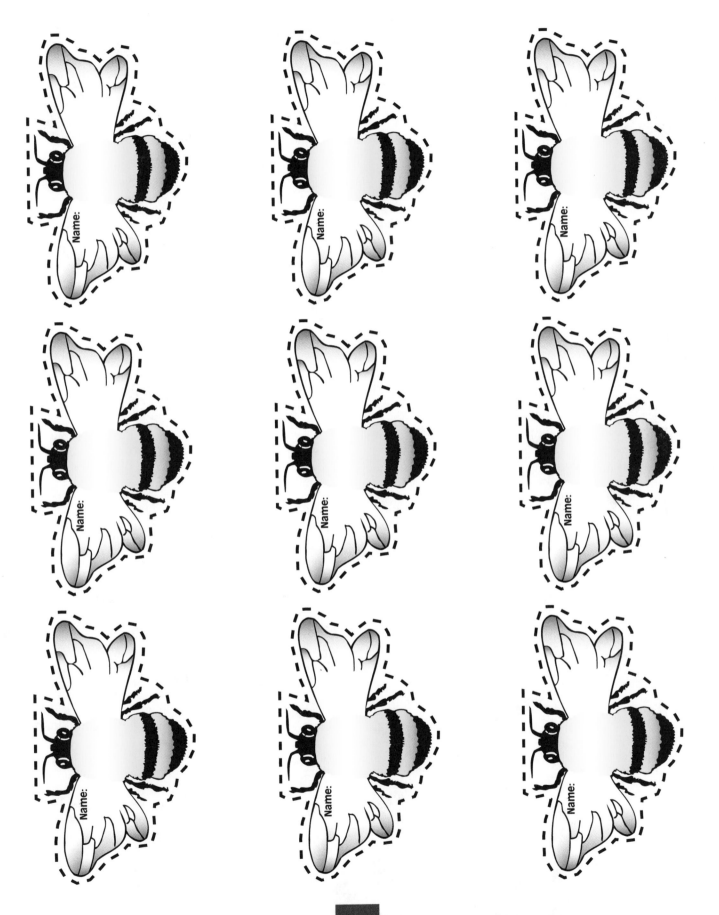

How to Plan Your School Year • EMC 779

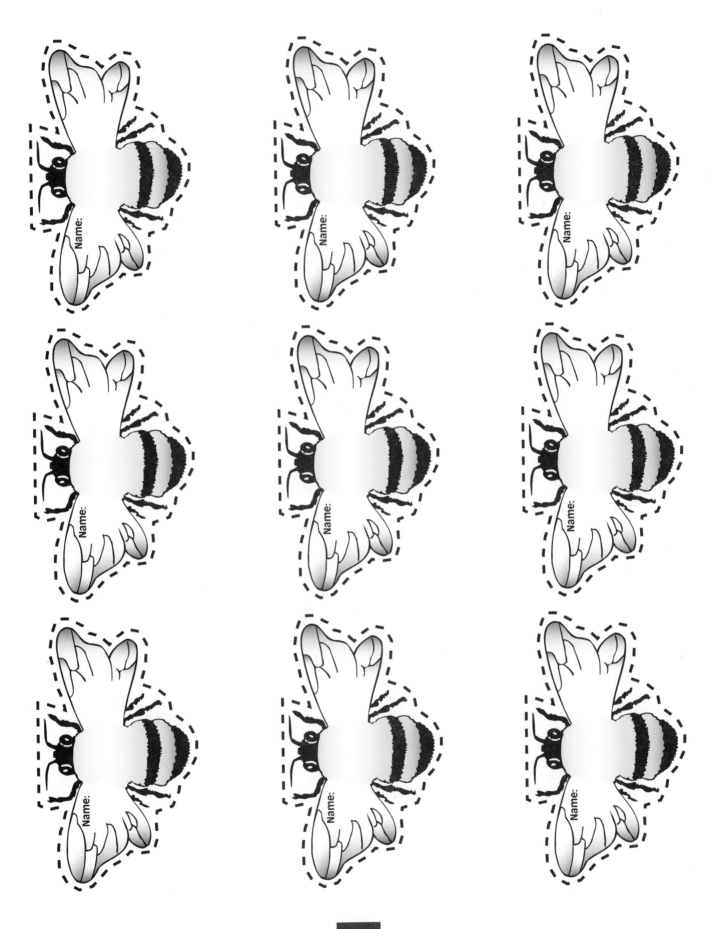

How to Plan Your School Year • EMC 779

Star Cutouts

How to Plan Your School Year • EMC 779

Shuttle Cutouts

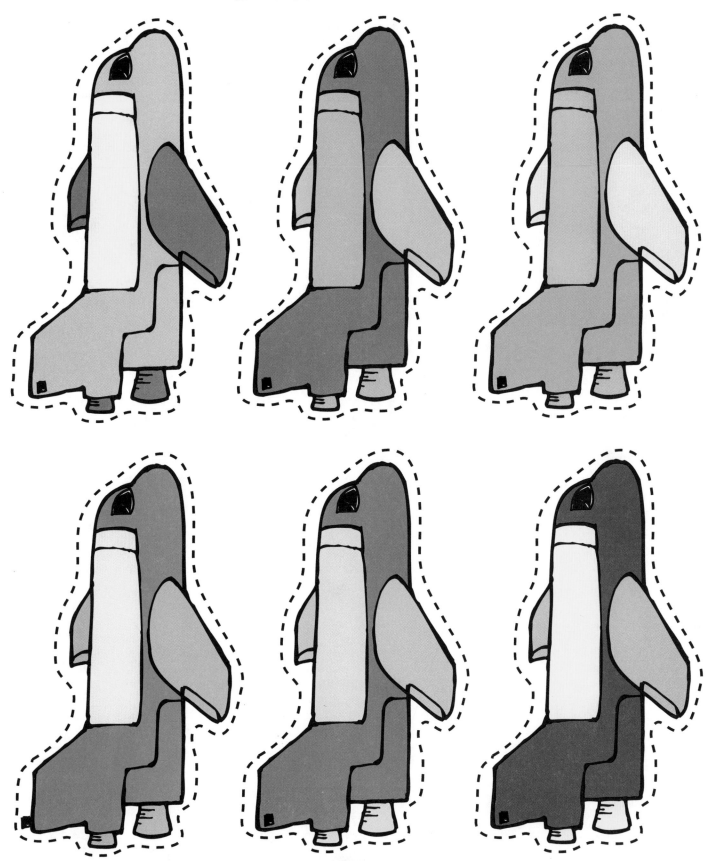

How to Plan Your School Year • EMC 779

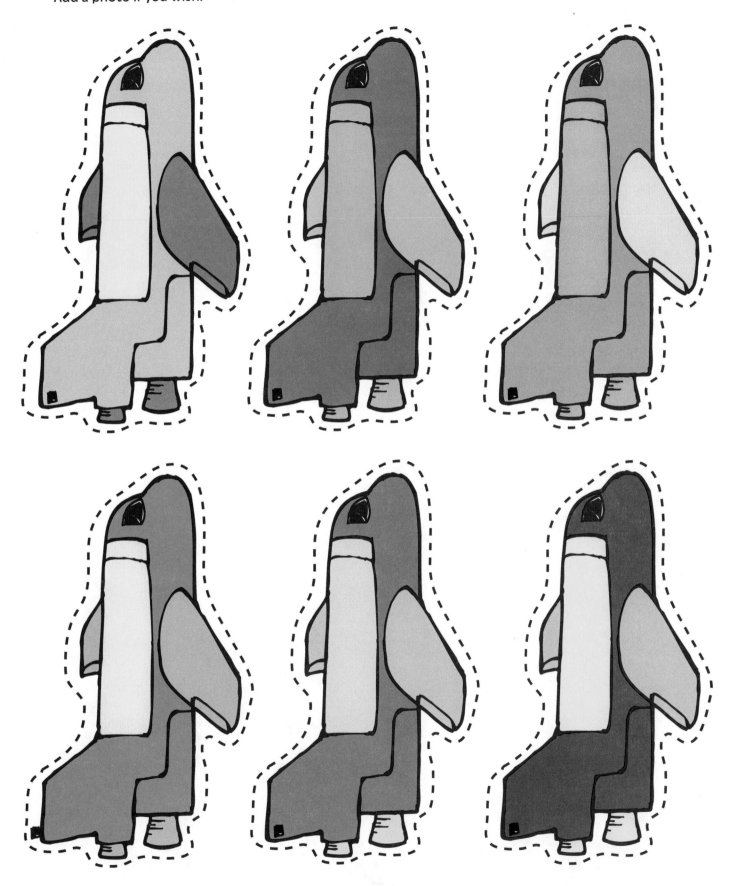

Note: Use with the Stars Job Chart on page 59. Label a shuttle for each student in your classroom. Add a photo if you wish.

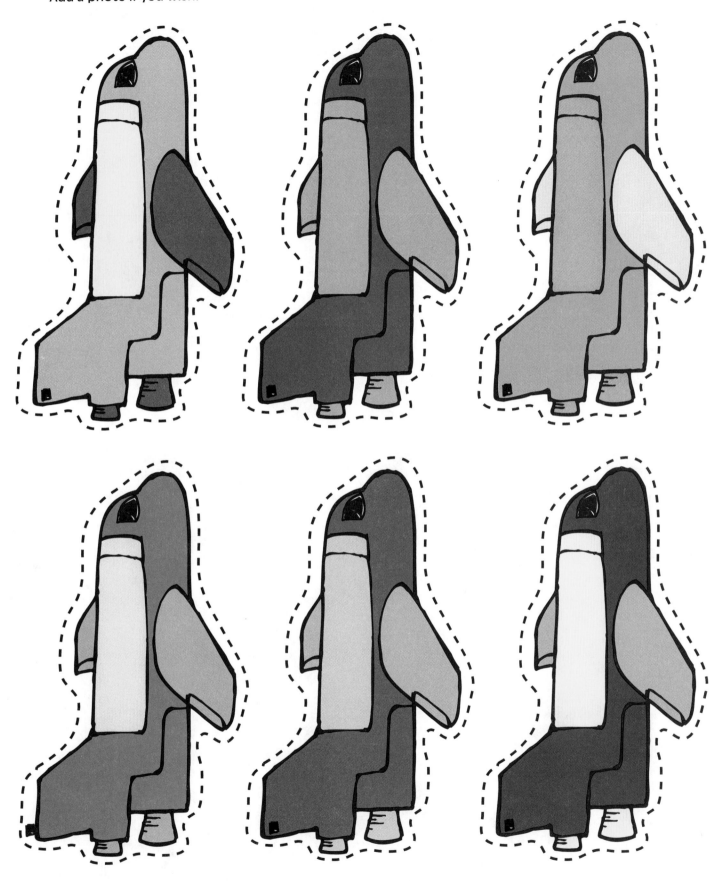

How to Plan Your School Year • EMC 779

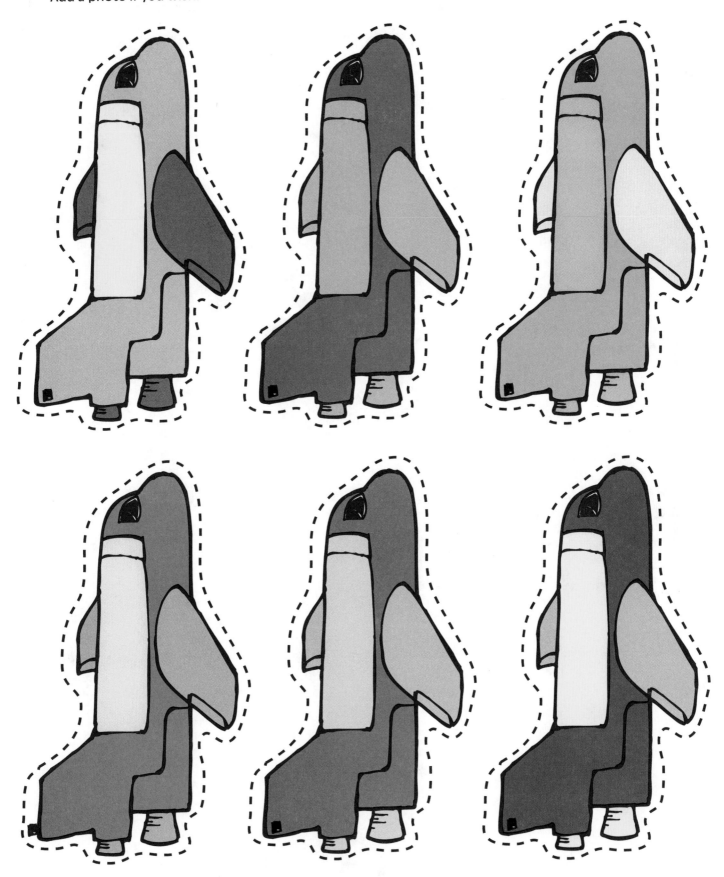

How to Plan Your School Year • EMC 779

Note: Use with the Garden of Helpers Job Chart on page 59. Reproduce one flower and two leaves for each job.

Flower Patterns

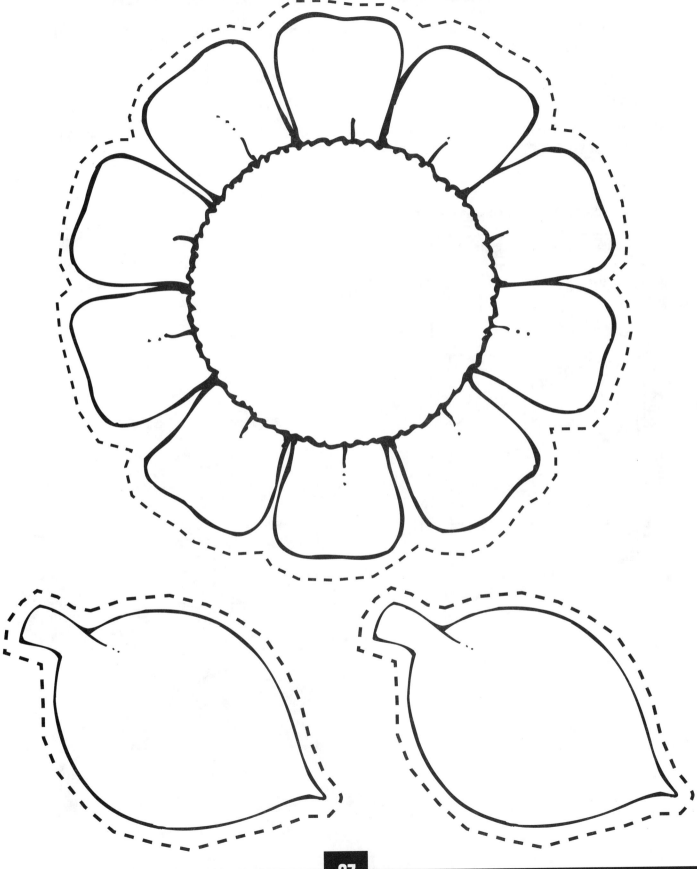

How to Plan Your School Year • EMC 779

When you display students' work in your classroom, you validate their efforts and their learning. At different times you may choose to

- show each student's interpretation of a single assignment
- have students choose the work that they want to display

Before school begins, put up the backdrop for your displays. Leave the background in place all year. Change work displayed often.

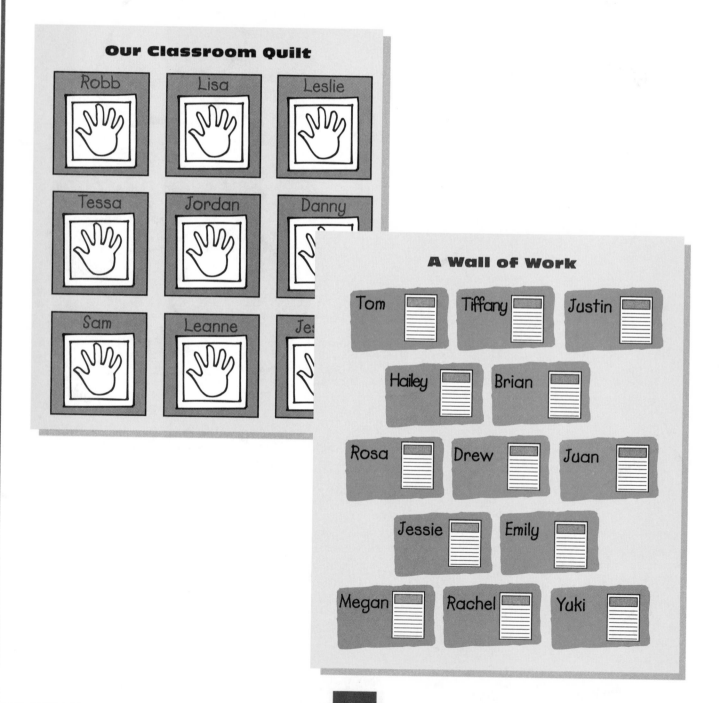

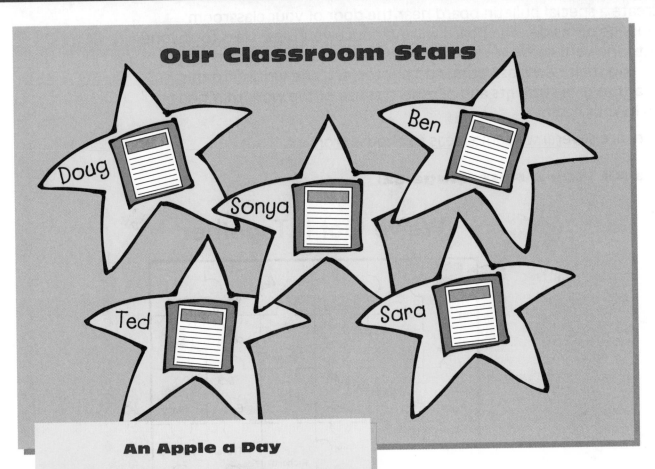

Our Classroom Stars

Doug

Sonya

Ben

Ted

Sara

An Apple a Day

Sonya   Tom   Vito   Jo

Helpful Hint

Mount student work on the same-sized paper each time you display it. Save the mounted samples. At the end of the year, bind them into a portfolio collection.

Bulletin Boards

Create a special bulletin board near the door of your classroom (outside or inside). The board will introduce your new class to anyone entering your room. It will give students a landmark when they're finding their new classroom. Add photos, art, and writing to this board to give students and parents a sense of the work that goes on in your room.

Here are several welcome ideas to choose from:

We All Play a Part (page 92)

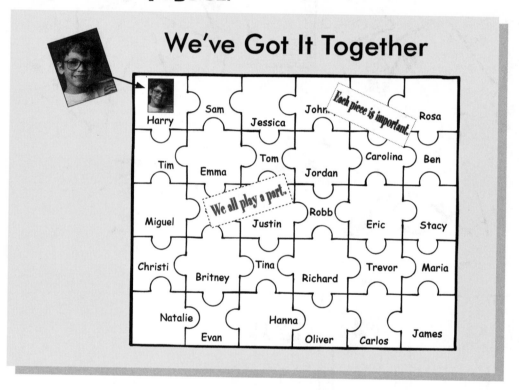

Trading Card Gallery (page 95)

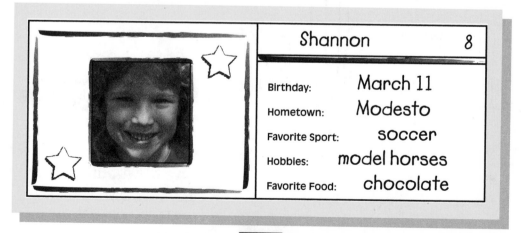

90

Who Will Be Here This Year? (page 97)

Before

Teeing Off for a Great Year (page 99)

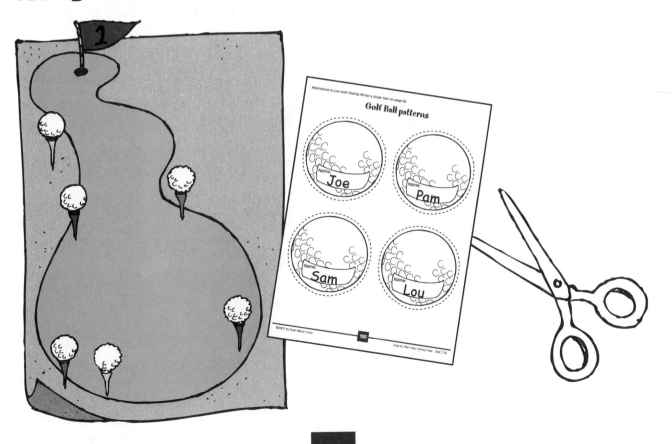

We've Got It Together

This provides a giant puzzle with one piece for each child.

What You Need

- puzzle pattern on page 93, with as many pieces as members of your class
- white butcher paper
- black marking pen
- overhead projector
- students' photographs
- signs on page 94, laminated and trimmed

We've Got It Together

What You Do

1. Cover the bulletin board with white butcher paper.

2. To make the puzzle:

    - Copy the puzzle on the photocopier.

    - Make a transparency of the copy.

    - Using your overhead projector, project the puzzle transparency on the wall. Move the projector until the size is correct.

    - Using black marker, trace the outline of each puzzle piece on the white butcher paper.

3. Write each student's name on a puzzle piece. On the first day of school, take each student's photo and add it to his or her puzzle piece.

4. If you have extra puzzle pieces, add additional information such as your room number, the year, your name and photo, the school name, etc.

5. During the first week of school, have students write a short description of themselves. Complete the puzzle by adding these descriptions to the puzzle pieces.

Note: Use with the We've Got It Together bulletin board on page 92.

Puzzle Pattern

Note: Use with the We've Got It Together bulletin board on page 92.

How to Plan Your School Year • EMC 779

Note: Use with the We've Got It Together bulletin board on page 92.

We all play a part.

Each piece is important.

Trading Card Gallery

This provides a trading card for each member of your class.

What You Need

- background—brightly colored butcher paper

- trading cards—pattern on page 96, reproduced for each student

What You Do

1. Cover the bulletin board with brightly colored butcher paper.

2. Add the caption—Trading Card Gallery

3. Have students complete trading cards.

   - Fill in information.

   - Add a photo or drawing.

4. Attach trading cards to the board.

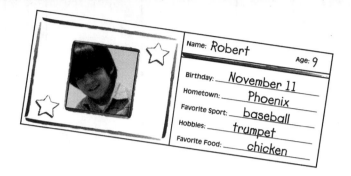

Note: When the cards are removed from the bulletin board, fold them in half and laminate them to create a permanent trading card collection.

How to Plan Your School Year • EMC 779

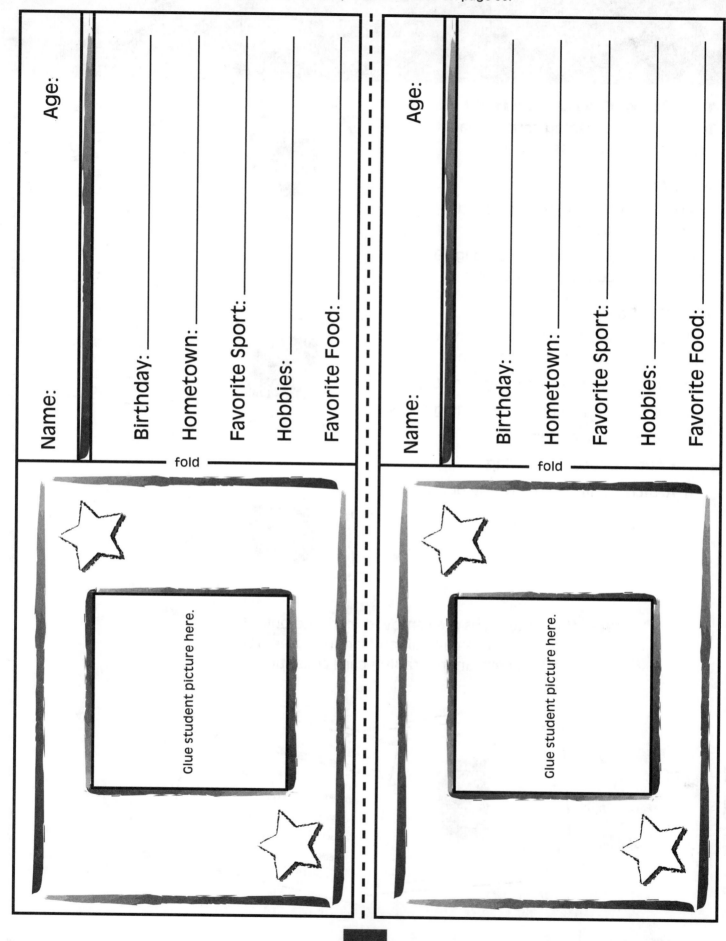

Age:

Name:

Birthday:

Hometown:

Favorite Sport:

Hobbies:

Favorite Food:

fold

Glue student picture here.

Age:

Name:

Birthday:

Hometown:

Favorite Sport:

Hobbies:

Favorite Food:

fold

Glue student picture here.

Who Will Be Here This Year?

This question is answered when the students arrive.

What You Need

- background—newspaper or butcher paper
- question mark and exclamation point—black posterboard
- student responses—

    colored construction paper

    response form on page 98, reproduced for each student

What You Do

1. Cover the bulletin board with newspaper.

2. Draw a giant question mark and an exclamation point on the black posterboard. Cut them out.

3. Pin the question mark in the center of the bulletin board.

4. When students arrive have them complete the pencil form on page 98.

5. Mount the pencils on colored construction paper.

6. Change the question mark to an exclamation point. Add student responses around the board.

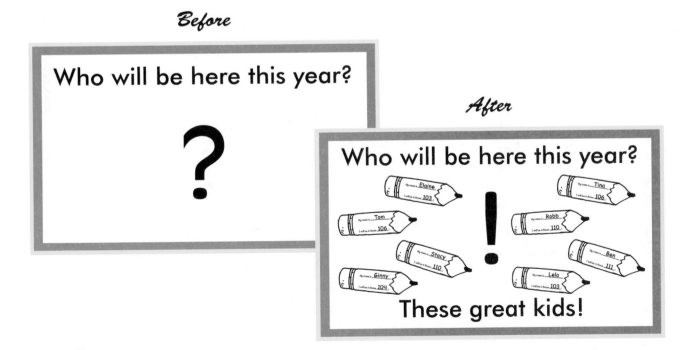

Before

Who will be here this year?

?

After

Who will be here this year?

These great kids!

How to Plan Your School Year • EMC 779

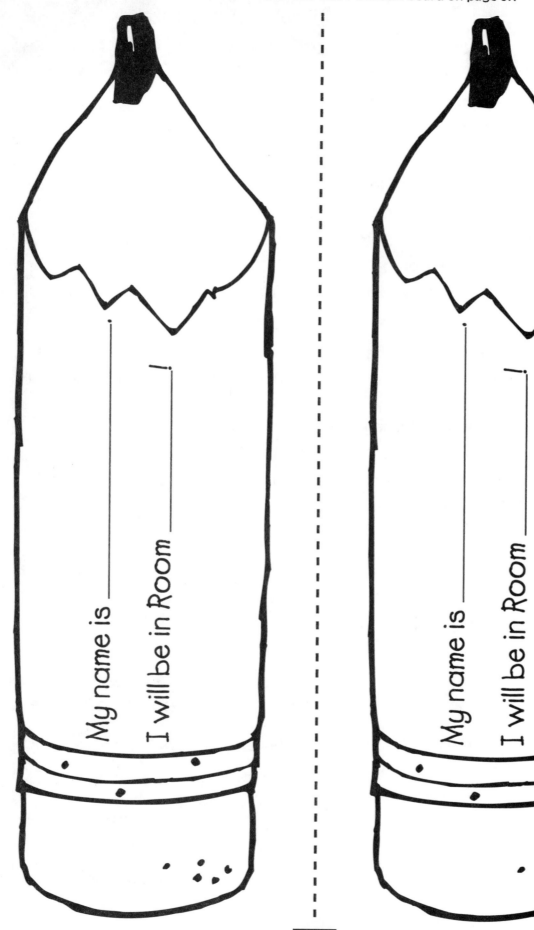

How to Plan Your School Year • EMC 779

Teeing Off for a Great Year

Put the focus on a class that's on the ball.

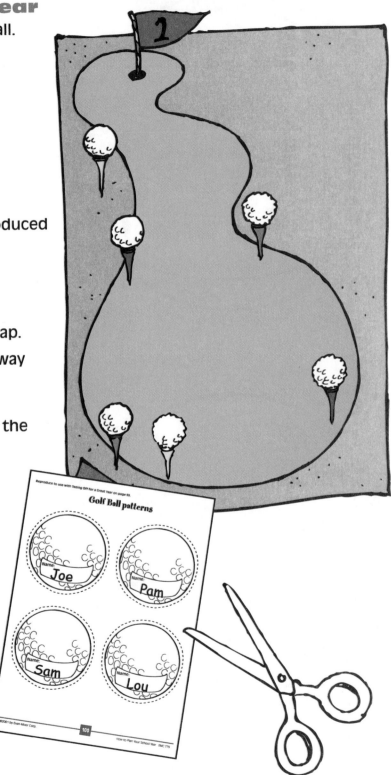

What You Need

- background—natural burlap
- golf fairway—green butcher paper
- striped straw
- scrap paper
- golf tees
- golf ball pattern on page 100, reproduced for each student
- photos of students (optional)

What You Do

1. Cover the bulletin board with burlap.

2. Cut a large irregularly-shaped fairway from green butcher paper.

3. Add a paper pennant to the straw to make a flag to mark the hole in the putting green.

4. Put golf tees around the edge of the fairway. Hint: Glue the tees to the green paper and allow to dry before stapling to the board.

5. Write students' names on the balls and put a ball on each tee.

   Optional: Add student photos to each ball. If you take a picture of the student sitting on a low wall and then cut out the student, it will look like he or she is sitting on the ball.

99

Golf Ball Patterns

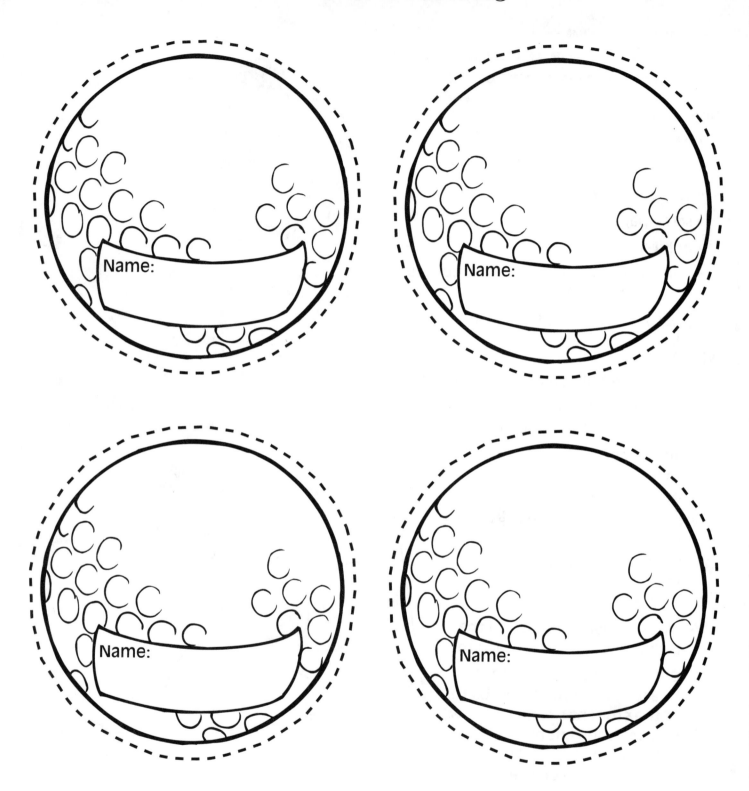

Name:

Name:

Name:

Name:

How to Plan Your School Year • EMC 779

Tags, Passes, and Checklists

■ Learn each student's name quickly.

■ Know where every student is.

■ Keep track of who has done what.

This section provides patterns for name and desk tags, full-color passes, and suggestions for using student checklists.

Contents

Name tags and desk or table tags will help you keep track of students during that crucial first day and beyond. Whether you attach the desk tag to the desk or let students pick up the tags from a table and choose their own desks, you will find the tags invaluable. They will help you connect names to faces. Use them over and over when students go to specialists, go on a field trip, or when guest speakers come to class.

Pages 103–106 provide four options for name and desk tags.

1. Reproduce the patterns.

2. Add some color.

3. Mount the reproduced patterns on construction paper or tagboard.

4. Fill in students' names.

5. Laminate tags.

6. Punch holes for safety pins or yarn.

Helpful Hint

Always make extra tags (a minimum of 5!) for possible last minute additions to your class. You will be able to correct any misspellings or nickname problems on these extra tags. Laminate on the spot with a few pieces of clear contact paper or laminate blank tags and use a permanent marker to add the name.

102

Puzzle Piece Name and Desk Tag

How to Plan Your School Year • EMC 779

Apple Name and Desk Tag

Anna

Anna

How to Plan Your School Year • EMC 779

Space Shuttle Name and Desk Tag

How to Plan Your School Year • EMC 779

School Bus Name and Desk Tag

Jenny

Jenny

106

Think about the procedure you will use to excuse students to use the bathroom.

Carry-with-You Passes

Provide a pass. You may want to provide both a boy's pass and a girl's pass. A student picks up the pass and carries it to the bathroom. The pass is replaced when the student returns. Special Considerations:

1. Passes should be durable and waterproof. Plastic cookie cutters work well.

2. Clips that attach to clothing or yarn circlets so that the pass may be worn as a medallion, keep hands free for washing.

On-the-Desk Passes

Provide a plastic shape or a sturdy stuffed animal. A student picks up the pass and places it on his or her desk, then goes to the bathroom. When the student returns, the pass is returned to its storage area. Special Considerations:

1. The pass should be big enough so that you can easily see it.

2. Students must remember to return the pass to its spot when they return from the restroom.

Sign-out Sheet

Provide a clipboard with a sign-out sheet and an easily-read clock. A student writes his or her name and records the time. When the student returns, he or she records the time again. Special Considerations:

1. Attach a pencil to the clipboard and keep it sharp.

2. Teach students how to write the time before expecting them to use this system.

107

Check with your colleagues to see whether your school has an established policy for students using the hallways during the school day. If not, establish your own pass system.

- Laminate the passes on pages 109 and 111.
- Discuss appropriate use of the passes with your class.
- Find a convenient and readily visible place to keep the passes and a way to keep track of whether a pass is being used and by whom.

Computer Pass

Room _____

Office Pass

Room _____

Library Pass

Room _____

Helpful Hint

Give students an occasional fresh air break. Take the long way to the library by walking out one side of the building and in the other side, sit outside to read a book, or visit the same spot on the playground to see how it changes over a month's time.

Note: Laminate these passes and use them.

Bathroom Passes

Computer Passes

How to Plan Your School Year • EMC 779

Note: Laminate these passes and use them.

Office Passes

Library Passes

How to Plan Your School Year • EMC 779

Checklists

Create a checklist using your class list. Use the spreadsheet program on your computer or reproduce the blank checklist on page 114. Fill in student names and make several copies.

Checklists will help you remember who did what! Here are some ways to use your checklist:

- Enlarge one list, laminate it, and post it on a magnetic board. Have students move circle magnets to show that they have arrived and to indicate whether they are eating school lunch.

- Hang one of the class lists by the doorway to use for fire drills. You can take it with you as you go out the door.

- Post a checklist in learning centers. Have students check their names after they have completed the activities.

- Set a checklist beside your in basket. Have students check off their names when they put their papers in the basket.

- Pass out checklists to class members. Pose a specific question, such as *How many people are in your family?* or *How many pockets do you have?* Have students interview each other and record the information on the checklist. Use the data to create graphs and word problems in math.

Database

In addition to the student checklist, prepare a student database either on your computer, in a card file box, or both. Include basic information for each student:

- name
- nickname
- address
- phone number
- parents' names
- allergies
- birthday

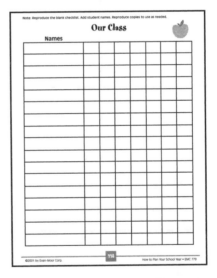

Note: Reproduce the blank checklist. Add student names. Reproduce copies to use as needed.

Our Class

Names

Helpful Hint

Labeling the hooks on the coat rack makes it easy to identify a student's coat. Designate space for lunch boxes and wet and cold weather gear. Being organized keeps the mess to a minimum.

Our Class

Names

How to Plan Your School Year • EMC 779

Take time to evaluate all the preparations you have made.

- Sit in different areas in your room. Check to make sure that there is a clear view of the chalkboard.

- Move from one work area to another. Is there a realistic traffic pattern?

- Mentally conduct an activity that requires students to move about. Are there any logistical problems?

- Are storage areas for supplies and student work in place?

- Do the bulletin boards and other decor convey a feeling of friendliness and welcome?

- Have you made up name tags, desk tags, and passes?

- Have you made copies of the student checklist?

- Is there an area for parents and volunteers?

115

Planning Your Curriculum

- Prior planning prevents poor performance!

- Long-range planning will help your year unfold smoothly.

- Plan and organize now to establish continuity in your instruction.

This section includes tips that will keep you focused on curriculum objectives.

Contents

In addition to planning the time slots that daily instruction will fit into, you will need to outline the specific skills to be taught during the year and include them on a yearly master calendar.

- Reference your school or district benchmarks or standards. If they are not available, outline the specific skills you need to teach this year for each curriculum area.

- Do a general plan of the units you want to include in the school year. Write the units on the calendar.

- Mark all the dates on the calendar that affect your program. Include:

    parent-teacher conferences
    vacations
    grading periods
    field trips
    guest speakers

- Once you have created a general plan for your year, add to the calendar as the days and weeks go by. Schoolwide activities and grade level events will change as the year moves forward. Classroom events will be scheduled as your class actively engages in learning.

- Record specific resources that are particularly helpful. Save your planning calendars from year to year.

- Reproduce the calendar page on the following page. Make one for each month that you teach. Choose the best way to use the pages in your planning:

    Place them in a binder with your standards.

    Tape each month's calendar to a folder. Collect resources and activities inside the folder for that month.

    Mount them on a bulletin board or file cabinet so you have a quick reference as you look ahead.

Month:

Monday	Tuesday	Wednesday	Thursday	Friday

Introducing Yourself and Your Classroom

■ Are you curious about your new students?

■ Do you suppose your students are curious about you?

■ Set the stage for a successful first day by making contact with each student before school starts.

This section suggests options for making that all-important initial introduction.

Contents

Send a Letter or a Postcard

It's always fun when you find something in the mailbox. It's even better when that something explains an important event like the first day of school.

- Be enthusiastic.
- Tell something about the first day of school for students to anticipate.
- Tell something about the room that they can use for identification.
- Tell something about the year ahead.
- Relate a question you will ask them on the first day, and ask them to think about an answer.
- Tell them you can't wait to meet them.

Stamps are expensive; check with your school to see if they will post the letters for you.

See the sample letter on page 121 and the postcard on page 122.

Make a Phone Call

If sending a letter isn't your style, phone each of your students. Speak briefly to them.

"Hi, Jose. This is Mrs. Norris. I'll be your teacher this year at Meadow School. I'm looking forward to meeting you at the Open House. When you come to our room you can choose a desk and we'll put your name tag on it. Do you like to sit in the front, in the middle, or at the back? Tell me about what you've been doing over the break. It was great talking with you, Jose. Be ready to tell me what you want to learn this year when you come on the first day. See you soon. Bye."

Do a Home Visit

Some teachers do a home visit to each of their students' homes. They meet with the student and the student's family and establish a valuable rapport. This is a time-consuming process, but establishes at the outset that you intend to work with the family and student to provide the best possible educational opportunities.

Keep your visit low-key and positive. Focus on learning about the student. Tell some of the exciting learning experiences you have planned for the year.

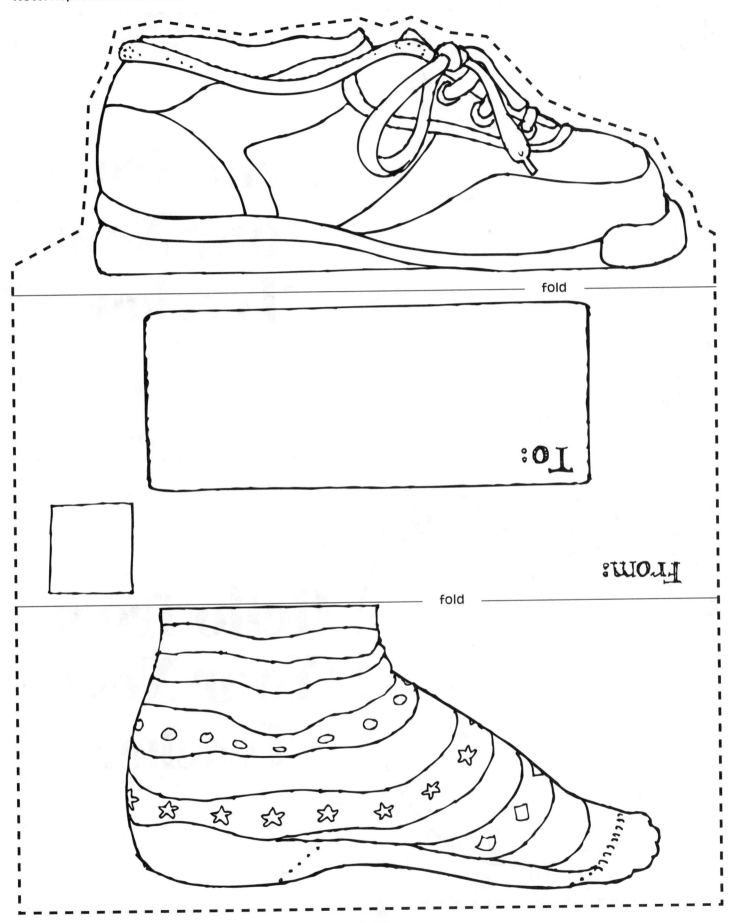

fold

To:

From:

fold

How to Plan Your School Year • EMC 779

Note: Reproduce these postcards on colored card stock. Write your message on the back and mail.

Hello from Your New Teacher

Hello from Your New Teacher

The First Week of School

■ What you do and say during the first few days sets the tone for the year.

■ Involve students in creating a classroom where everyone learns.

■ Build a support team of school staff and parents.

This section offers suggestions for developing standards and procedures, building class unity, and establishing good parent communication.

Contents

Make the first day of school one that students will remember. Be sure to plan time for the following important items.

Greet the Class

Welcome your class warmly and let them know that you are looking forward to a year of exciting learning. Do something active—sing a song, read a poem, tell about yourself, or introduce the class mascot.

Attention Signal

Decide on a signal that will be used only for this purpose. For example:

- "Give me five." or
- "Attention, please." or
- Raising your hand in a particular manner.

Explain what the signal means.

- *"Give me five* means—Eyes on me. Ears listening. Feet still. Hands quiet. Voices off."
- *"Attention, please* means you stop whatever you are doing and look at the person giving the signal."
- "When my hand is up, your eyes are on me and your voice is quiet."

Practice giving the signal and having the class respond. Repeat this practice throughout the first day and week.

Expectations

Outline your expectations in positive language.

"Does anyone know what *expectations* are? That's right, expectations are the things you believe will happen. I have three expectations for our class this year:

1. We will learn together.
2. We will recognize that we are all unique individuals and respect our differences.
3. We will be positive and polite."

Establish Rules

Pages 155–159 provide important guidelines for implementing a set of rules for your classroom.

Routines and Procedures

Start on day one to establish important routines that will help your classroom run smoothly throughout the year. Page 126 provides suggestions on what routines you might consider.

How to Plan Your School Year • EMC 779

Student Learning Goals

Ask what students want to learn this year. You'll be surprised at the expectations they have. Make a list and post it somewhere in your classroom. Refer to it periodically. Check off the things you have learned.

Locate Restrooms

Walk the class to the restrooms so that everyone knows where they are. (This also provides the opportunity to practice your line-up routine and hallway rules.) Explain the procedure students must use when they wish to use the restroom.

Get to Work

It's important that the first day be productive. During the first period of the day, be sure to conduct some type of lesson—solve a math problem or read a story together, or do an art project that will be displayed in the room.

Tour the School

Prepare a chart of the places you will visit (special classes, cafeteria, office, library, etc.) and the staff members you will meet. This is another opportunity to practice your line-up routine and hallway rules. Fire drill procedures might be discussed at this time also. Point out where the class goes during a drill.

Teach Something New

When your students get home, walk through the door, and hear, "What did you learn today?" they need a ready answer.

- For kindergartners and first-graders, this might be to recognize a single word.

- For second- or third-graders, it might be how to solve a special math problem.

- For fourth- or fifth-graders, it might be the definition of an unusual word.

125

Classroom Routines and Procedures

Many times the classroom offers the first structured, organized environment that a child experiences. Students will be at ease knowing exactly what to expect in your classroom. An organized classroom, brought about by a well thought out set of standards and procedures, sets students up for success. Routines give them a foundation and comfort zone where they can learn and prosper.

Routines

To create a productive classroom, develop a routine for every student-related movement, situation, or activity—no matter how insignificant the activity may seem. You don't need to do every single routine on the first day, but you will need to introduce many.

Sharpening a pencil is a minor activity. But when seven students get up to sharpen their pencils at the same time, get into an argument as to who is first, and break the handle off in the scuffle—all while you are in the middle of teaching math—a minor activity becomes a major event. Don't leave anything to chance or you will be taking a big risk!

So—

- Make step-by-step charts for all the routines you will put into place.

- Practice some of the routines on the first day. Repeat the routine several times with positive praise—*Wow! Look how well you walk in a line and it's just the first day of school!*

- Add more routines as you need them. Don't forget to discuss and practice each routine before you expect it to be done correctly.

You'll want routines and procedures for the following:

sharpening pencils

getting a drink

using the bathroom

lining up

getting materials

accessing centers

how to use free time

turning in homework

hanging up coats and book bags

Helpful Hint

Bulletin Board Hint

A magnetic pin container is invaluable! It eliminates spills and encourages student involvement in posting information.

126

The Class as a Team

It is important that the students in your class work together. They need to feel comfortable and safe. They need to see themselves as a caring group that supports and challenges members to realize their potentials.

Students learn by interacting with teammates. They

- communicate their ideas,
- defend their answers, and
- teach concepts to others.

But this does not happen automatically. Just as an orchestra needs a conductor, the teacher must play an active role in creating harmony in the classroom.

One way of assuring success is to incorporate team-building activities into the first week's schedule. Team building prepares students to work cooperatively. It helps focus student energy and enthusiasm for positive academic outcomes.

Time Well-Spent

Team-building activities develop team spirit and cohesiveness, foster on-task behavior, and work out the kinks within the class before academic instruction begins.

A team-building activity provides opportunities to unite to solve a problem. The possibilities are endless. Activities can be passive or active, silent or verbal, simple or complex, a few minutes long or last for a whole class period. The following are just four examples of good first week team-building activities.

For more information on team building and cooperative learning see Cooperative Learning on pages 238–255.

Primary Activities

Who Is It?

1. The class sits in a circle on the floor or on the playground.

2. Have each student give his or her name. Repeat the names to clarify pronunciation if the student is hard to hear.

3. Now the memory game begins. The student on your left says, "I'm _____."

4. The next student says, "I'm _____ and this is (names the first student.)"

5. Each subsequent student names those who came before. Since you are last, you name everyone in the class.

I'm Sue. This is Pete.

Spider Web Questions

You will need a large ball of heavy twine for this activity.

1. The class sits in a circle on the floor or on the playground.

2. Ask the question, "What is your favorite _____?"

3. Name a student in the circle. Hold onto the free end of the twine. Roll it across the circle to that student.

4. The student catches the twine, answers the question, names another student, holds the twine, and rolls the ball to the second student.

5. The game continues until all students have answered the question.

Alphabet Lineup

1. Have students line up in alphabetical order.

2. Start with *A*. Students with names beginning with *A* stand and arrange themselves in alphabetical order.

3. Continue with each letter.
   Note: In the process of doing this lineup, you will have created a real graph of names starting with each letter. You may want to record the results.

128

Intermediate Activity
Who Could It Be?

The classic icebreaker where participants mill around a room and find others who fit certain descriptions is a great way to get to know one another.

1. Reproduce the form on page 130 for each student. You may want to white out some of the facts and use ones specific to students in your class.

2. Establish ground rules for the activity.

   • Use six-inch voices. (Voices that can't be heard farther than six inches away.)

   • Practice good manners.

3. Students move around the room, exchange forms, and sign their names next to an appropriate description. Each student may sign another student's grid only once.

4. The object of the activity is to complete the grid.

Reproduce this grid for each student in your class.

Who Could It Be?

brown eyes	has braces	wears glasses	likes fishing
is the oldest child	plays an instrument	can do a cartwheel	likes broccoli
has a dog	is the youngest child	has slept outside	can sew
wears sandals	has five pockets	has natural curly hair	can blow a bubble
likes hats	rides a bike	read a book last night	can swim
loves ice cream	speaks Spanish	likes pickles	has a dimple

Helpful Hint

Several students might make a master grid by filling in every possible correct answer. This master grid could become the center of a bulletin board. Post student biographies and photos around the grid.

129

Who Could It Be?

brown eyes _____	has braces _____	wears glasses _____	likes fishing _____
is the oldest child _____	plays an instrument _____	can do a cartwheel _____	likes broccoli _____
has a dog _____	is the youngest child _____	has slept outside _____	can sew _____
wears sandals _____	has five pockets _____	has naturally curly hair _____	can blow a bubble _____
likes hats _____	rides a bike _____	read a book _____	can swim _____
loves ice cream _____	speaks Spanish _____	likes pickles _____	has a dimple _____

How to Plan Your School Year • EMC 779

Acknowledge with your students the important roles that all staff members play within the school.

1. Talk about school staff members. Ask:

   - How does what the custodian does affect our classroom?

   - How does what the librarian does affect our room?

   - How about the nurse? The lunchroom manager?

2. Invite school workers into your room to describe their responsibilities.

3. Create a flip chart or permanent bulletin board of school workers. This important reference may include names, job descriptions, and photographs. When you ask a student to take a note to or invite a specific staff member to your classroom, have the student first locate that person on the school worker board.

4. Upper-grade students may interview workers and write the descriptions as an individual writing assignment. Primary students may complete the descriptions as part of a class writing project.

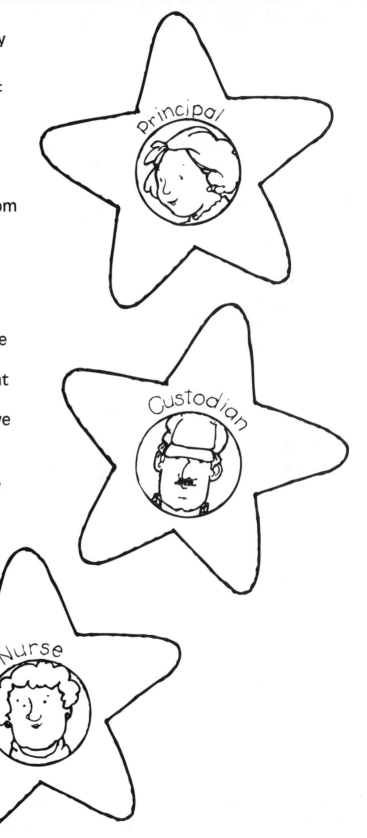

131

Dear Parents,

We've had a great beginning.

Here are some of the exciting things we did this week.

from
Room

One way to approach planning the first day is to organize the day around a read-aloud book. Eric Hill wrote the wonderful book *Where's Spot?* Early readers love this flapbook and soon read not only the answers, but the questions as well. Organize your first day, including a school tour, around this book.

Introductions

- Greet students and choose seats.

- Take roll. Ask a question and have each student respond with an answer. Two possibilities are, "Have you ever played Hide and Seek?" and, "Do you have a dog at home?"

- Discuss and create expectations and class rules.

- Introduce Spot. Read *Where's Spot?*

School Year

- Plan a tour of your school. Cut out the bone notes on pages 137 and 139. Post one bone at each spot you will visit on your tour.

- Put the two notes from Spot on page 135 in separate envelopes. Arrange to have the first note delivered to the class.

- When the note is delivered, read it. Then suggest that your class walk through the school to find Spot.

- Stop at each location. Introduce your class to the school workers and explain what you would do in that spot. For example, "This is the nurse's office. If you hurt yourself at school or start feeling sick, the nurse will help you."

- If students don't "spot" the posted bone, point it out.

- After the tour, read the second note from Spot. (It was left in class while you were on the tour, of course!) This is a great time for a snack of cookies in the shape of bones.

Read-Aloud

- Read *Spot's First Day at School* by Eric Hill.

- Discuss what you know about Spot and his friends.

Math—Bone Math

- Reproduce the record sheet on page 134 or purchase mini dog biscuits for counters.

- Give each student 8 mini dog bone biscuits for counters or have them cut out the bones on the record sheet.

- Model the use of the counters to find all the combinations that make another number.

Language—A Class Book

- Cut book pages. You will need one 8" (20 cm) square and one 2" (5 cm) square for each student.

- Ask students, "Where do you think Spot is now?"

- Students respond by each drawing a page for a class book. They glue the small squares to the pages and write their answers underneath the flaps.

How to Plan Your School Year • EMC 779

Bone Math

How can you make ☐ ?

Write the ways here.

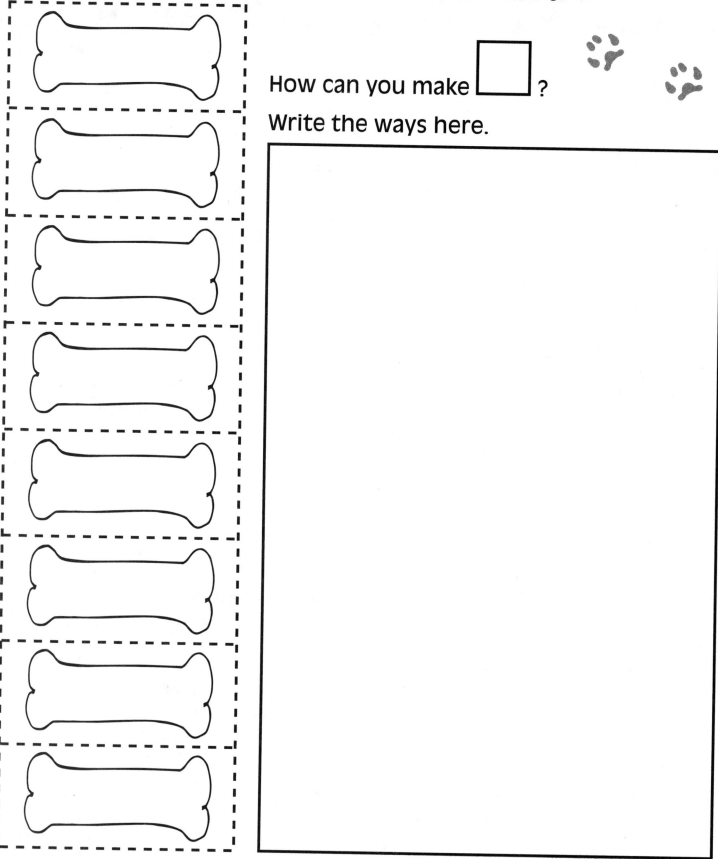

Dear Boys and Girls,

What a great school you have! I like it here. There are interesting places and interesting people. Maybe I'll see you around.

Love,

Dear Boys and Girls,

Sorry I had to leave before I met you. It's been a busy day. Have a great time learning new things. I hope to see you soon.

Love,

How to Plan Your School Year • EMC 779

Note: Post these bones in each location you will visit on your school tour.

Bones

I was here. I think this is an important place to know about.

See you around.

I was here. I think this is an important place to know about.

See you around.

I was here. I think this is an important place to know about.

See you around.

I was here. I think this is an important place to know about.

See you around.

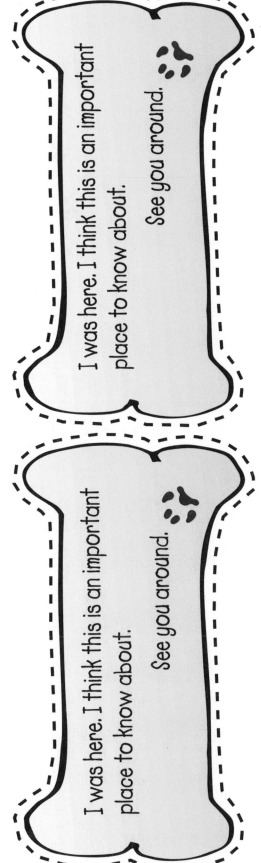
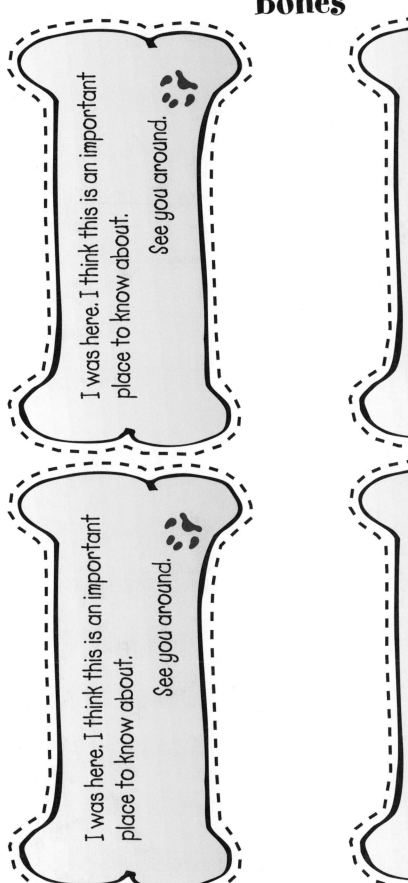

How to Plan Your School Year • EMC 779

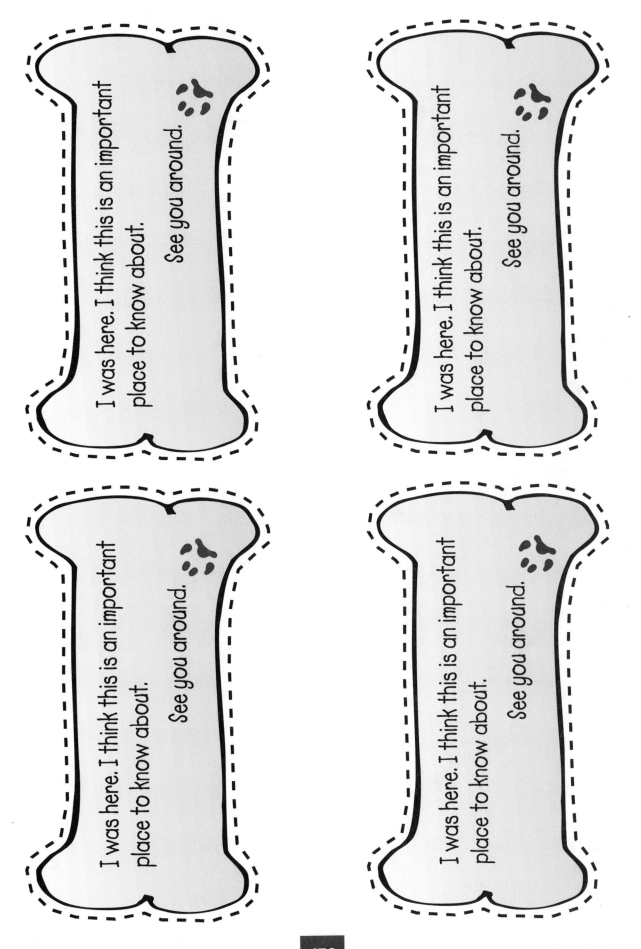

I was here. I think this is an important place to know about.

See you around.

I was here. I think this is an important place to know about.

See you around.

I was here. I think this is an important place to know about.

See you around.

I was here. I think this is an important place to know about.

See you around.

How to Plan Your School Year • EMC 779

One way to organize the first day is to focus on a theme. Since you and your class are opening the door on the school year, why not begin the day with "Knock, Knock," "Who's there?"

Introductions

- Greet students and choose seats.
- Introduce yourself.
- Establish expectations and class rules.

Learning About Each Other

- Reproduce the door pattern on page 142.
- Give each student a blank door. Have students decorate their doors to reveal their personalities and interests. They should not write their names on the doors.
- Students write a description of their doors, explaining the symbols they have used.
- Display the decorated doors. Share the descriptions. See if students can match doors and descriptions.

Learning About School Helpers

- It is important to realize that each member of the school team has an important job that contributes to learning success.
- Reproduce the interview form on page 143. Let your staff know that your students will be doing the interviews. You may even want to set up appointments.
- Have students interview staff members to find out what their responsibilities are. Students may report results orally or in written form.

- Create a book or bulletin board display with the information.

Math—Think Math

- Reproduce the activity sheet on page 144.
- Have students complete the page showing two different solutions. The activity may be done in pairs or small groups.
- As a class, compare the solutions. Record all correct solutions on enlarged copies of page 143.
- Issue a challenge to find still more solutions.

Language—Spelling Skills

- Reproduce the activity sheet on page 145.
- Write the words Knock, Knock on the chalkboard or overhead.
- Ask students what they know about the words. They may say the k is silent, the ck works together to make one sound, the o is short, it's one syllable, or it means "to rap." Acknowledge their responses and explain that there are many words in the English language with silent letters.
- Have students work independently or in small groups to identify the silent letters on the activity sheet.

Language—Quotation Marks

- Reproduce the knock-knock jokes on page 146.
- Use the jokes to teach the use of quotation marks.

141

Note: Reproduce this door pattern to use with the Learning About Each Other activity on page 141.

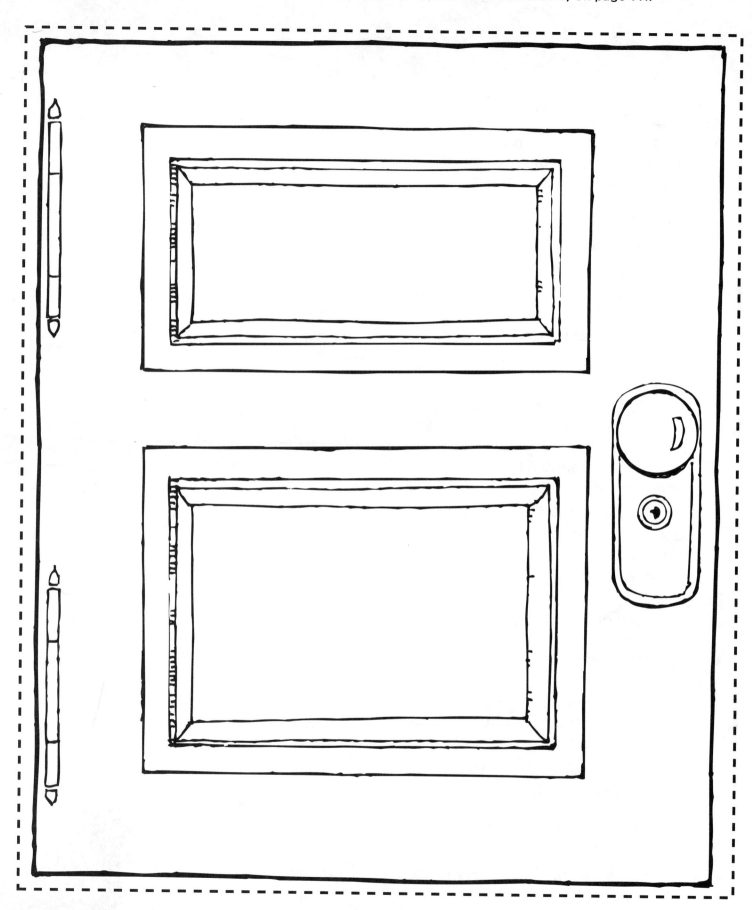

How to Plan Your School Year • EMC 779

Knock
Knock

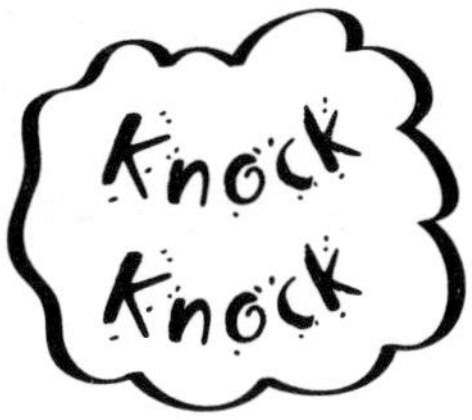

Name _____

Name of Job _____

Where Found _____

Responsibilities

• _____

• _____

• _____

• _____

• _____

• _____

• _____

Best Part _____

_____

_____

Worst Part _____

_____

_____

Interesting Moment _____

_____

_____

_____

Name: _____

Think Math

Use the digits 1 through 9 to complete these number sentences. Use each digit only once in each solution.

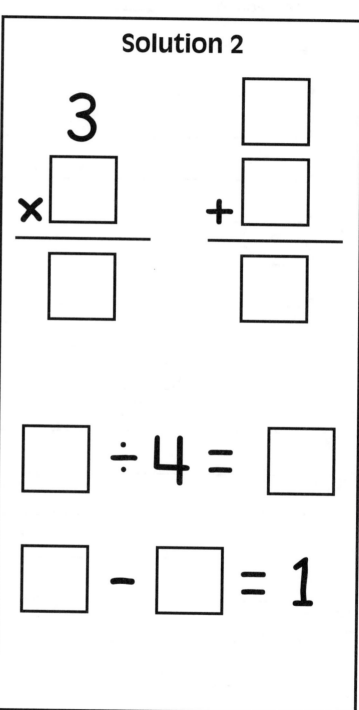

Solution 1

$$3 \times \square$$
$$\overline{\square}$$

$$\square + \square$$
$$\overline{\square}$$

$$\square \div 4 = \square$$

$$\square - \square = 1$$

Solution 2

$$3 \times \square$$
$$\overline{\square}$$

$$\square + \square$$
$$\overline{\square}$$

$$\square \div 4 = \square$$

$$\square - \square = 1$$

How to Plan Your School Year • EMC 779

Name: _____

Spelling

Knock Knock

Which of the bold letters are silent? Circle them.

1. **wr**estle   4. cli**mb**   7. ha**l**f   10. **is**land

2. an**sw**er   5. ta**lk**ing   8. whi**stle**   11. desi**gn**

3. o**ft**en   6. **kn**ot   9. toni**ght**   12. scra**tch**

Circle the five misspelled words below. Write them correctly on the lines.

_____

_____

_____

_____

This summer I went camping on an iland near my home. I carried everything I would need in a napsack. When I reached the ranger station, he was talkin about which campsites were still available for camping tonite. I asked about a campsite near the lake. His anser was to nod his head and point to a trail going up to the left.

Finish the story on the back of the page.
Remember to think about words with silent letters.

     How to Plan Your School Year • EMC 779

Who's Talking?

Quotation marks and paragraphs help the reader to know who's talking. Rewrite the following jokes. When the speaker changes, start a new paragraph. Add the quotation marks.

Knock, knock. Who's there? Dwayne. Dwayne who? Dwayne the tub. I'm drowning.

_____

_____

_____

_____

Knock, knock. Who's there? Boo. Boo who? Please don't cry.

_____

_____

_____

_____

Classroom Management

■ Students need and deserve an orderly and organized setting.

■ Managing a classroom is like running a country. The leader must create an environment where the inhabitants are safe, content, and encouraged to prosper.

■ Excellent classroom management is crucial for student success.

This section has suggestions for maximizing student participation, establishing a discipline plan, trouble-shooting problem situations, and more.

Contents

Students look at teachers as role models and mentors. It is important that you project an appropriate image. What you DO makes more of an impression than what you SAY. You can tell children to aim high, but let them see you shooting for the stars and they'll be right behind you ready for the journey skyward.

Maintain Composure

Demonstrate for students that the best way to deal with challenging situations is to remain calm and level-headed.

One teacher told the story of an enraged parent bursting into the classroom, shouting and using profanity. The teacher remained calm, notified the office, escorted the parent into the hall, and returned to the classroom. After a brief discussion with the students on ways to handle conflict, the teacher continued the existing lesson. Students were able to remain calm because their teacher was calm.

Be Organized

It is difficult to complain to students about their messy desks when the teacher's desk is piled with papers, coffee cups, books, and part of a sandwich from the week before. It is also tough to fault off-task students when a poorly structured lesson has left them with idle time. Organize your environment from your desk to your lesson schedule. Display your organization by posting agendas, To Do lists, and planning calendars.

Be Warm and Caring

An empathetic teacher creates empathetic students. Sarcasm and belittling statements create hostility. Think about a favorite teacher from the past, and chances are it was a teacher who made you comfortable with kindness.

Be Honest

Teachers should admit when they do not know an answer. This can become a teachable moment: "That's a good question, Carlos, but I don't know the population of China. I do know exactly where to look to find the answer though." Students learn that it's okay to not know every answer, that even adults need to search for answers, and that resources are available to help them.

Admit if you forgot to grade an assignment you promised to return, if you are in a grumpy mood, or if you don't find a particular piece of literature interesting. An honest teacher earns the respect of the students.

Praise Students

Don't miss an opportunity to compliment your students when appropriate. Research shows that this increases the likelihood of more good behavior. It also encourages children to compliment their peers.

148

Show Your Love of Learning

It is vital that children see adults who are excited about learning. Tell students about the books and magazines you read at home. One teacher shared with the class that he was always reading at least three books. At the end of the day, students asked if they could check out more than one library book so they too could read three books at a time! Bring in newspaper or Internet articles to share, talk about classes you take in the evening, and show pictures from your vacations. Make it clear that learning is an exciting process that continues throughout life.

Demonstrate Respect

Respect is contagious. Let students catch you being respectful toward others, especially in challenging situations when you disagree with someone or when someone is being disrespectful to you.

Maintain Authority

Gaining respect from your students requires that you establish the leadership role in the classroom from day one. The first hour with your students is crucial in establishing your presence in the classroom. Remember that old saying "You don't get a second chance to make a first impression"? Maintain a clear line of authority; being a pal with students can compromise your position. Keep a demeanor that is businesslike, but pleasant and supportive.

A good rule of thumb: Start out being stricter, and ease up after it is clear you are the one in control. It just doesn't work the other way around!

Be Fair

Let your actions be an example of the Golden Rule: Treat others as you would want to be treated. The opportunities are endless. Administer classroom rules and consequences equally, without exceptions for any particular student. Grade assignments by considering the ability of the child, the scope and importance of the work, and how the class scored as a whole. Pay heed to the amount of work you assign and the deadlines you set for students. Avoid comparing students to each other.

Be an Optimist

The classroom should be one place where students can expect a positive atmosphere. Show them how even hopeless-looking situations can present opportunities; teaching children to "turn lemons into lemonade" is a valuable life skill. Let them see you use a positive attitude, a strong spirit, and a sense of humor to meet life head-on.

149

Don't keep your expectations of the students a secret! Starting on the first day of school, state your expectations, why they are important, and how they can be met. While some of these may be reflected in your classroom rules, you should still review all of your expectations.

Create a Chart

Have your expectations in the first column already listed. Have students add to the list and help you complete columns two and three. The students buy into this concept when you include them in the process. (See the sample chart on page 151.)

Post the chart your class creates. Refer to it often. Praise students for meeting and exceeding expectations.

Assume That Your Expectations Will Be Met

One way of making this clear involves your discussions with students. Say, "I'm so happy I can expect excellent behavior in the cafeteria—you make me proud every time we go in there" or "I always know that the hallway outside our classroom is clean because of your efforts." These statements set the stage for the students. They know you have high expectations and that they have a reputation to live up to, and the situation remains positive as long as they comply.

Expectation	Importance	How We Do It

Helpful Hint

Phone a parent or send a note home to compliment a student who meets or exceeds expectations.

What We Will Do

Expectation	Importance	How We Do It
• Show respect for other students and for their property.	• This allows everyone to get along. • It keeps fights and arguments from happening.	• Refrain from name-calling. • Use the property of others only with their permission. • Treat people like we want to be treated. • Listen until others are finished speaking.
• Show respect for teachers	• This is an important part of being a good citizen. • It makes learning easier.	• Arrive on time for school. • Do our assignments. • Make our best efforts. • Obey classroom rules. • Ask permission.
• Be respectful in the cafeteria.	• This makes the cafeteria a more pleasant place. • This keeps it looking nice.	• Say "Please" and "Thank you" to the cafeteria staff. • Speak quietly. • Pick up our trash. • Pick up litter.
• Respect our school.	• This makes us proud to be students here.	• Keep the bathrooms neat. • Help keep our classroom organized.

Instruction that is interesting and appropriate is a vital component in maintaining discipline. Well-planned lessons leave no time for misbehavior. Keep the following guidelines in mind.

Be Prepared

When it comes to teaching a lesson, "winging it" often results in a crash landing. A good lesson requires careful advance planning. Have lesson plans, equipment, and materials ready and waiting.

Demonstrate "With-it-ness"

If you are always alert during your lessons (with that third eye in the back of your head helping out), you can catch misbehavior before it materializes. If you notice a student who begins to whisper to another, say, "I know this class understands how important it is to be respectful when another person is speaking." This keeps the atmosphere positive, reinforces good behavior, and squelches a potential problem in an anonymous way.

Create Interactive Lessons

The attention spans of students seem to shrink every year. If students sit idly while the teacher drones on and on they will lose interest, misbehave, or enter that trancelike state that's hard to shake.

Make learning interactive. Ask for predictions and personal examples relating to the topic. Rather than telling them all the information, allow them to discover some of it on their own. Vary your presentations, include videos, exposure to literature, music, guest speakers, and hands-on activities. Make learning come alive: instead of just talking about the Oregon Trail, have students pretend to plan for the trip, then create a journal of someone who may have taken the journey.

Pacing

You know the feeling—you're sitting in a movie that is going nowhere and the minutes seem like hours. Avoid this scenario in the classroom by keeping a close eye on the pacing of lessons. Divide each lesson into varied parts such as reading, writing, listening, and a hands-on activity. Assign a time estimate to each of these parts. As you teach the lesson, stick to these time estimates. Not only are you better able to complete the lesson, but your students will be engaged. If students look restless at any point, adjust your approach to bring them back. Be sure that transitions between parts of the lesson are smooth so that no time is wasted.

Stay on the Subject

Students respond best when a lesson is structured and focused. Don't confuse them by straying off the topic. Refrain from talking about the new fund raiser in the middle of reading class. Minimize outside interruptions that are within your control.

Students learn more when they participate actively. Use teaching strategies that encourage student participation.

Simple Techniques for Everyday Discussions

- When you ask a question, give students "think time" to compose an answer. Let them know you will always count to fifteen after asking a question and that you expect everyone to be ready to answer at that time.

- Ask a question and have every student respond with a thumbs up or thumbs down.

- Provide small dry-erase boards or number cards and have every student show you the answer to a problem.

- Have students share their ideas with a neighbor (pair share) before you call on an individual.

Clock Partners

Create 12 potential pairings in advance by having students fill out a clock partner form.

- Reproduce the clock partner form on page 154 for each student.

- Each student asks another student to be his or her clock partner for a specific hour. The two exchange forms and sign their names in the appropriate spots.

- Continue until the forms are full. Students tape the forms inside their work folders.

- When you need to divide the class into groups of two, you simply say, "Find your 2 o'clock partners." Students consult their forms and move quickly to work.

Helpful Hint

Instructional centers and cooperative learning are two additional ways to maximize participation. See pages 172–255.

Name: _____

My Clock Partners

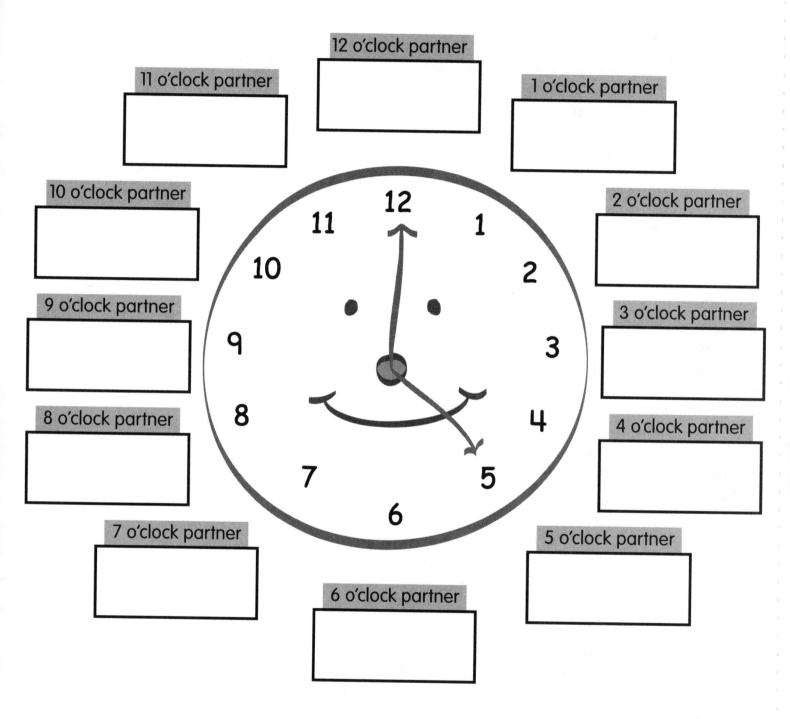

11 o'clock partner

12 o'clock partner

1 o'clock partner

10 o'clock partner

2 o'clock partner

9 o'clock partner

3 o'clock partner

8 o'clock partner

4 o'clock partner

7 o'clock partner

5 o'clock partner

6 o'clock partner

How to Plan Your School Year • EMC 779

New teachers are often surprised at the amount of time they spend disciplining students. It is frustrating when discipline-related activities overshadow academic time, when you lose your temper, or when one student leads the whole class into chaos.

A classroom of out-of-control students is a classroom where learning is unlikely to happen, and where the teacher goes home every night with a pounding headache. There is no single correct answer to solve this daunting problem of discipline.

Fortunately, there are ways of making sure that students are on-task rather than misbehaving. A comprehensive approach that encompasses rules, consequences, rewards, as well as instruction, is required. Think of it as your battle plan. You have to train the troops, develop strategies, create a plan of attack, practice, and learn from past mistakes. And if your discipline plan is effective, it may become the first battle plan ever that leads to no battles whatsoever!

The first step in managing a country or a classroom is to establish a clear set of rules. Keep the following guidelines in mind.

Develop a General Set of Rules

In many schools the faculty creates a general set of rules either for each grade level or for schoolwide use. While individual teachers may customize these general rules using their own language or even by adding an additional rule, there is consistency among classrooms. These basic rules might include:

- Use appropriate language.
- Keep your hands, feet, and objects to yourself.
- Raise your hand to speak.
- Respect school property and the property of others.
- Have materials ready on time.

Have a few students demonstrate what it looks like to follow a specific rule. Students will then have the rule in words and actions.

Limit the Number of Rules

Students can easily be overwhelmed when faced with a litany of rules. Limit the number of rules for primary grades to three or four. For intermediate grades, four or five rules are sufficient.

Make the Rules Positive

Rules stated in the negative, "Don't call out in the classroom," tell students what NOT to do, but give no hint as to what they SHOULD do. Greeting students with a list of negatives hardly keeps the atmosphere positive. Instead, state your rules positively. Instead of saying, "No running in the hallway," say, "Walk in the hallway." Instead of, "Don't hit your classmates," say, "Keep your hands to yourself."

Create Clear and Concise Rules

Students are more likely to follow rules they can easily understand. Keep them short and to the point: "Raise your hand to speak" is more effective than, "During class when the teacher is speaking, when you are in line, or during schoolwide assemblies, do not talk unless you have permission from a teacher or an administrator."

Also make sure that each rule focuses on a more generic theme as opposed to details. That way one rule can apply to many situations. A more generic rule like "Respect school property" covers a whole host of topics, such as littering, graffiti, textbook care, etc.

Develop Rules with Students

Even though you may have a generic set of rules in mind before school starts, give the students a role in developing the final classroom list. Guide them in creating the rules by saying, "What kind of rule could we write that would help us keep our school clean?" *Respect school property.*

Have a group of students artistically write the rules on poster-size paper. When students have an active part in the process they feel a sense of ownership and accountability.

Post the Rules

Give your list of rules a prominent place in the classroom—front and center—so it is convenient to refer to them throughout the day.

Focus on a Single Rule Per Day

Before jumping into academics each day, choose one rule from the list to highlight for the day. Model the rule, or better yet have students model the right way to follow the rule. Keep an ongoing chart of ways to follow each rule.

Respect school property looks like:

- clean, neat bathrooms
- litter in the garbage cans
- textbooks in good condition

Create a way of rewarding the class if they follow the rule that day and verbally praise them as you see them complying. Just spending a few moments on this process emphasizes the importance of the rules and keeps the list fresh in their mind.

156

Mention the Rules Daily

Another way to stress the importance of the classroom rules is to mention them consistently. Relate them to topics of study: *The Mayflower Compact is a lot like our classroom set of rules.* Or *The character in our story would not be in trouble if he had followed which one of our classroom rules?* Let the class discuss ways in which following the rules would have made a real-life situation better.

Give Recognition When the Rules Are Followed

Make a concerted effort to mention any signs of compliance with the rules. *I was so impressed with the way everyone said "please" and "thank you" to the cafeteria staff today. What a mature, polite group of students you are to follow our rule that says "Respect all teachers and staff."*

A reward system tied to the rules is also an effective way to encourage compliance. See pages 162–169 for more on rewards.

Our Class Rules

1. Respect yourself and your classmates.

2. Respect school property.

3. Respect all teachers and staff.

After developing classroom rules, the next step in your discipline plan is creating consequences. The consequences tell what happens when the rules are broken. They act as a deterrent by giving students concrete reasons to follow the rules. Keep the following suggestions in mind as you develop consequences.

Develop a General Set of Consequences

As with the rules, work with others on the faculty to create a general, schoolwide set of consequences. This allows for consistency among classrooms, even if individual teachers customize the consequences.

The list of basic consequences may include:

Step 1—verbal warning

Step 2—student describes in writing what happened and how it can be avoided in the future

Step 3—a phone call or note to the parents

Step 4—privileges are taken away

Step 5—student is referred to the office

Relate Consequences to the Severity or Frequency of the Infraction

Consider developing a total of three to four consequences that increase in severity. Begin with a consequence for minor infractions (e.g., a verbal warning if students yell out in class) and lead up to more severe consequences (e.g., referral to the office for fighting or for students who break numerous rules in one class period). Note the examples given above which range in severity from minor to major. Some major infractions, like fighting, should result in an automatic referral to the office.

Ask Students to Help You Develop the Consequences

Just as you include students in the process of developing classroom rules, involve them in the creation of the consequences so they buy into the concept. Again, use your clever teacher skills to guide them so they come up with the consequences you already had in mind.

Post the Consequences with the Rules

The classroom rules are most effective when the consequences are listed close by.

Apply the Consequences Fairly

If students break a rule, apply the consequence as it is written. Avoid altering a consequence for one student or allowing students to bargain with you to lessen the penalty. This type of inconsistency only leads to problems. Be neutral when you explain the consequence; being sarcastic or mad puts the student in a defensive position.

Recognize a Student After a Consequence Is Completed

If a student misses recess because of a rule infraction, spend a moment discussing the situation with that student. Ask, "Was it difficult to stay inside when all the others were outside? Did you learn from this experience? What could you do next time to avoid this situation?" Be sure to compliment the student for completing the consequence—"I'm proud of the mature way you handled this consequence" or "I can tell by the mature way you handled this that you'll avoid breaking this rule in the future."

Helpful Hint

Be consistant and fair. Keep your consequences simple and straightforward.

Many schools have simple techniques that facilitate enforcement of classroom rules. Use some of the techniques below. Create your own. Keep discipline under control with simple structures that make the rules/consequences process smoother.

Green-Yellow-Red Chart

In a central classroom location, post a "pocket" (like the ones in the front of library books) for each student. Write the name of each student on the pockets. In each pocket place a green, a yellow, and a red card that stick out of the pocket by at least three inches. Place the green card in front, followed by the yellow card, and finally the red card.

Students remain on "green" if they avoid breaking rules that day. If they break a rule, they move their green card to the back of the pocket so the yellow card is showing. Further rule infractions lead to the red card. You may choose to add an additional colored card or two to each pocket to create more of a hierarchy for rule infractions and consequences.

At the end of each day, record the color for each student, either on a chart you post or on a document you keep at your desk. Determine an appropriate reward system. For example, students who remain on green for a week will get 15 extra minutes of free time on Friday. Create photocopied certificates to send home each week— *Congratulations! Your child stayed on green all week!*

Cool-Off Corner

Choose a desk or table away from the rest of the students to create a Cool-Off Corner. Post a list of three or four questions at this location:

Which rule did you break?

Why did the class create this rule?

How could you have handled this situation in a different way?

How do you feel? How does the other person feel?

This is the spot where a student can go as a consequence of breaking certain rules or a certain number of rules.

It might work like this: You decide that any student who reaches a red card on the chart goes to the Cool-Off Corner. The student is expected to take a sheet of paper and a pencil to the designated location. Give the student a maximum of five minutes to answer the posted questions. The student places the completed paper on your desk. This entire process should happen without your involvement and without interrupting the class.

For the early grades, when writing skills are less developed, students could draw their responses on a form that has questions.

Discipline Log

Use a simple form to document rule infractions. Store the forms on a clipboard and make the student who broke the rule responsible for recording the information. This documentation is valuable for use in parent meetings or for report card comments. Just knowing that infractions are recorded emphasizes to the students that you take this process seriously.

Helpful Hint

Don't forget to let parents know when a student has a good day. A special telephone call or note can make a big difference.

161

Consequences are balanced with rewards. Rewarding those who comply with the rules is an incentive for them to continue their good behavior. Remember, a reward system does not need to be elaborate or complicated. It is not necessary to reward students with "things," but in some situations and with some students "things" sometimes provide the motivation necessary to establish a classroom management system.

Avoid over-rewarding students; this waters down the incentive to do well. Also avoid using candy as a main reward. You don't want to create trained seals that only respond to a treat tossed their way.

Consider using one of the following reward strategies.

Spell the Reward

Let the class choose one reward they can earn for good behavior. This might include popcorn and a movie, a field trip, a class celebration, or a pizza party. Explain that they can earn this reward one letter at a time. Here's how it works:

At the end of each day, determine if the class as a whole deserves recognition for their behavior that day. If so, write the first letter of their reward on the board— "P" for Pizza Party. Every day add another consecutive letter if their behavior was appropriate. If their behavior was not appropriate, a letter is not written. Do not erase a letter as punishment; you should not take away what they already earned. When the reward is completely spelled out, let the celebration begin!

You are not necessarily responsible for financing the rewards. If you notify parents in advance, students can bring in treats, music, games, videos, or a money contribution. Local businesses are often good sources for financial contributions.

Hint: Whatever reward the class chooses, make sure it has at least 10 or more letters in its name ("Pizza Party" rather than "Pizza"). Otherwise the rewards may happen too frequently, becoming less of an incentive and more of a routine.

162

Reward Raffle

On Friday issue raffle tickets to each student based on their compliance with the classroom rules that week. Determine how many tickets to give each student.

If you use the "Green-Yellow-Red Chart" described on page 160, award one ticket for each day the student stayed on green. Or award three tickets to students with no infractions and one ticket to those who broke a rule. The goal should be more tickets for those with the best behavior.

After writing their names on the raffle tickets, students place them in a bag. Then five or six tickets are chosen from the bag and prizes awarded to those lucky winners. Prizes don't necessarily have to be purchased.

- Ask local businesses for donations. (pens, fast-food coupons, samples)

- Create coupons of your own. (free hint on a test, no homework, first in line, sit at the teacher's desk for an hour, computer time, lunch with the teacher/principal, take home art supplies) Reproducible coupons are provided on pages 168 and 169.

See additional free or low-cost reward ideas on page 167.

Fill the Can

Place a small empty coffee can on your desk. When you observe examples of classroom rules compliance, drop a token into the can. Use pennies, dried beans, plastic chips, marbles, or anything else that makes an audible sound as it drops in. At the end of the day, drop four or five tokens into the can if the overall behavior was appropriate. When the can is full, reward the class. As described in "Spell the Reward," allow the class to determine the reward, search for ways of financing the reward, and avoid removing tokens already placed in the can.

Rocket to Rewards

Find a spot in the classroom where there is free wall space from floor to ceiling. Cut out and laminate the rocket on page 165. Tape or pin it to the wall, with the bottom of the rocket resting on the floor. Use pieces of masking tape to mark every six inches from floor to ceiling above the rocket. On a paper star write a reward that the class determines. Post the star at the top.

At the end of each day, move the rocket up six inches if you feel the class followed the rules. If they didn't, the rocket remains where it is. Don't move it down. When the rocket reaches the star, the class receives their reward.

Note: There are many variations on this theme: a monkey climbing to get a banana, a thermometer, a bee flying toward a flower, and a bird flying to a nest. If horizontal wall space is available, try a ship sailing to a lighthouse, a car driving to a house, or a rabbit running to a carrot. Choose a theme appropriate for your class.

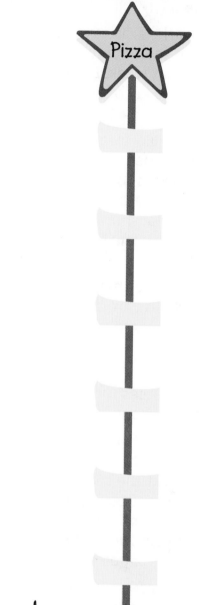

How to Plan Your School Year • EMC 779

Note: Cut out the rocket. Mount it on posterboard and laminate it. Use it with the Rocket to Rewards activity on page 164.

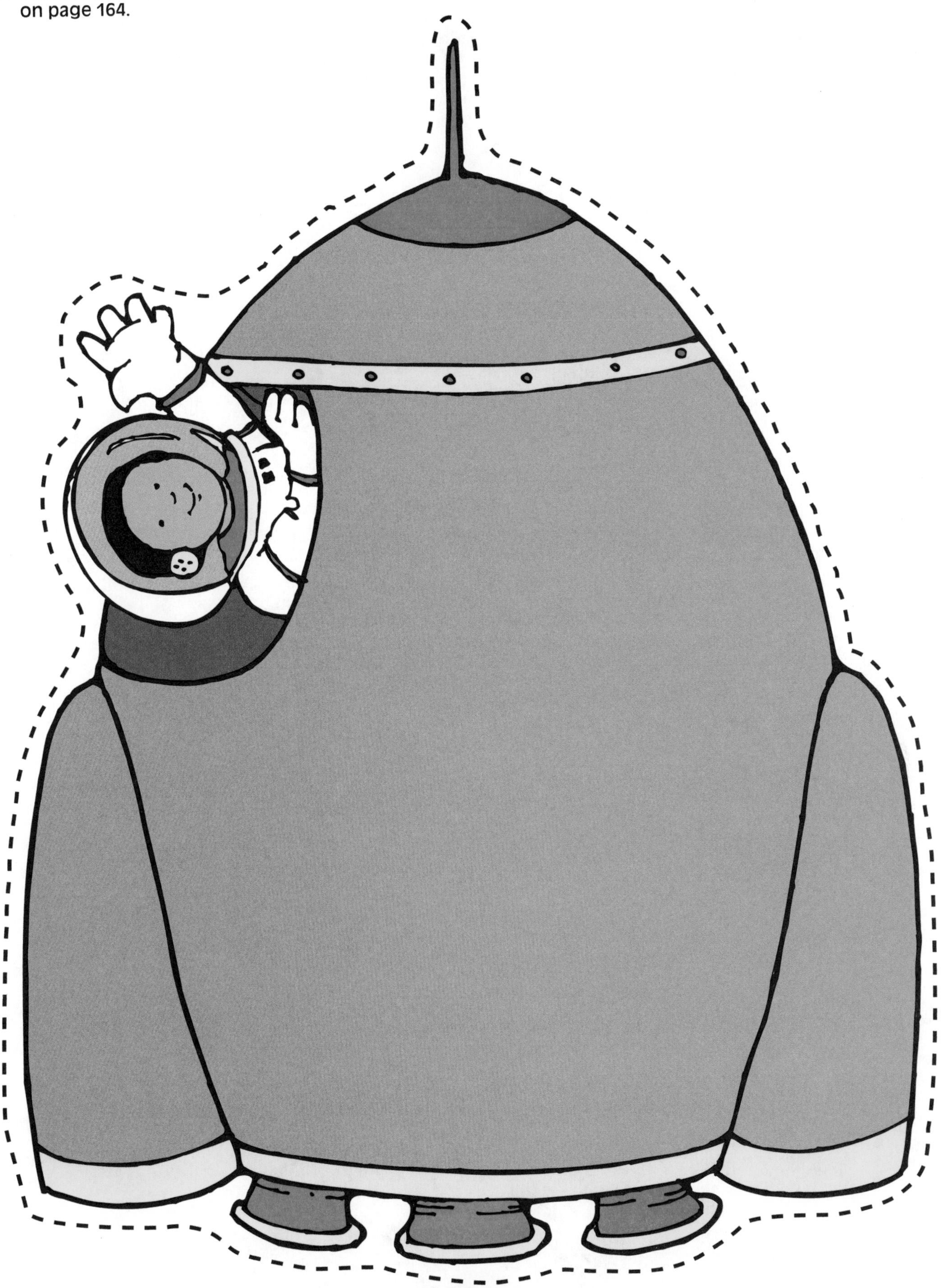

Individual Student Rewards

- Positive note or phone call home
- Student's picture posted on the Student of the Week bulletin board
- Pass to use colored chalk on the sidewalk
- Pass to bring a CD or cassette to play for the class
- Pass to the media center or computer lab
- First in Line coupon
- Home art kit overnight pass
- Pass to sit on the couch or beanbag chair
- Extra computer time
- Good behavior certificate
- Pass to sit at teacher's desk
- Permission to check out 3 books from classroom library
- Lunch with the teacher
- Permission to use stamp and ink pad
- Pass to go to lunch 5 minutes early
- Pass to read to a younger child
- Lunch with the principal
- Helper for the Day badge
- Eat lunch with another class
- Pass to stay in at recess to play board games
- Pass to write on the chalkboard or dry-erase board
- Keep Good Citizen trophy or stuffed animal on desk
- Pass to use the overhead projector

- Coupon to choose a seat for the day
- No Homework coupon
- Pass to help gym teacher or librarian
- Bookmarks
- Pass to help in the office
- Teacher Assistant pass to help teacher with a special task, such as reorganizing room or preparing a bulletin board
- Delete 3 Questions on an Assignment coupon

Whole Class Rewards

- Hold a class session outside
- Eat lunch outside
- Read a story outside
- Watch a video
- Have a theme day like Hat Day or Backwards Day
- Celebrate with a pizza party (Ask students to contribute or ask for donations from local restaurants.)
- Have a class party (Ask students to bring the treats.)
- Take a field trip to a nearby park
- Invite a guest speaker to share his or her expertise and experiences

Reward Coupons

No Homework

Help the Librarian

Teacher's Assistant

Choose New
Seat for a Day

Do Only Half
a Math Assignment

Computer Time

Reward Coupons

Be First in Line

A Great Phone Call Home

Eat Lunch with the Teacher

Stay Indoors for Recess

Extra Center Time

Read to a Younger Child

How to Plan Your School Year • EMC 779

Classroom Management
Trouble-Shooting

Classroom rules, consequences, and rewards go a long way in managing student behavior. But for some types of misbehavior there are other, more specific strategies to consider. Use the following suggestions for dealing with particular types of misbehavior.

Problem: inappropriate clothing
Prevention: schoolwide dress code

Problem: student outside of classroom without authorization
Prevention: passes issued by teacher for any errands
students must have teacher permission to leave the room

Problem: student behind teacher's desk
Prevention: off-limit areas established by teacher

Problem: the domino effect—misbehavior spreading from one student to others
Prevention: teach students the advantages of ignoring bad behavior
more opportunities for rewards

Problem: late students
Prevention: a brief too-good-to-miss activity scheduled at the start of each day
tie timeliness to the reward system
call parents on the day the student was tardy
establish a routine for late students that minimizes disruption
- Put the late pass on the teacher's desk.
- Walk around the edges of the room to your seat.
- Quietly get your materials ready.

Problem: speaking out in class
Prevention: a rule requiring raised hands to speak
limiting questions asked to class as a whole
Think-Pair-Share strategy on page 242.

Problem: a student refuses to work
Prevention: call to parents
coordination with school counselor if problem continues
behavior contract
daily reports

Problem: a student brings computer games or toys to school
Prevention: the June Box—Confiscate inappropriate items students bring to school and place in a box to be returned on the last day of school.

Books

Big Bucks: A Creative Discipline System by Joanna Hazelwood; Maupin House Publishing, 1998.

The Caring Teacher's Guide to Discipline: Helping Students Learn Self-Control, Responsibility, and Respect by Marilyn Gootman; Corwin Press, 1997.

Classroom Discipline Solver: Ready-to-Use Techniques for Managing All Kinds of Behavior Problems by George Watson; Center for Applied Research in Education, 1998.

Positive Discipline: A Teacher's A–Z Guide by Jane Nelson, et al.; Prima Communications, Inc., 1996.

Setting Limits in the Classroom: How to Move Beyond the Classroom Dance of Discipline by Robert J. MacKenzie; Prima Publishing, 1996.

Teaching with Love and Logic: Taking Control of the Classroom by Jim Fay; Love and Logic Press, 1998.

Magazines

Educational Leadership Magazine (Available by joining Association for Supervision and Curriculum Development, 800-933-2723)

Education Week Magazine (800-728-2790)

Phi Delta Kappan (800-766-1156)

Teacher Magazine (800-728-2753)

Web Sites

URLs for Web sites change frequently. For online resources related to classroom management, go to the Product Updates link on our Web site.

- www.evan-moor.com
- click on Product Updates (link at bottom of home page)
- scroll to EMC 779 How to Plan Your School Year and click

Instructional Centers

■ Centers may be used as an integral part of your curriculum or as enrichment activities.

■ Centers may be used for exploration and discovery.

■ Centers may be used for practicing and applying skills that have already been taught.

This section includes ideas for center organization, as well as the directions and patterns for four portable skill centers, each with options for both primary and intermediate activities.

Contents

Make a folder for each center. Keep a copy of the tasks done at each center for each rotation period. File these copies in the appropriate folders. You are creating a great resource of activities to meet the needs of all your students. As you find center activities you think you might like to try in the future, file them in a "new possibilities" folder.

There are several ways to approach moving students through centers.

1. You may want to formally rotate students. Here are two ways to do this:

   - Write the name of each center on the pocket. Write student names on cards and place them in the pocket. Rotate cards with student names through the centers.

   - Organize students into groups. List the names of the students in a group on a large card. Write the names of the centers on your chalkboard. Post the card with student names under the center name. Move the cards as the students rotate.

2. You may prefer to allow students to choose which centers they visit. Provide each student with a tracking form, a name card, and a clothespin. They clip their name cards to a location at the center to show that they are working there. On the tracking form, fill in the centers that they visit until work at all centers has been completed.

Lost and Found Tub

A plastic tub placed beside the coat rack is a great lost and found container. At the end of a day, put any leftovers in the tub. Stray mittens, socks, and hats can be found easily when parents and students know where to look for them.

173

One effective way to structure centers is to base them on major areas of the curriculum and to maintain them, with minor changes, throughout the year.

A Writing Center

Maintain the writing center all year, changing a few things from time to time to reflect topics being studied. Provide a basic set of supplies: different kinds of paper, special pencils and pens, and writing assignments. Add new assignments and special supplies periodically.

A Math Center

Your math center should have several sets of manipulatives, stumper problems to solve, and practice activities that support current instruction. Tile math, geoshapes, Unifix® cubes, fraction kits, games, and other hands-on activities may be featured at different times.

A Reading Center

Always include a center for independent reading in your room. Include a bookcase, rack, or basket of books, soft pillows or chairs, and tracking and response forms. Each week take time to spotlight new books that you have added to the center.

An Art Center

Provide art supplies and project ideas. Then encourage your students to express themselves creatively.

A Science Center

The science center area is a great place to house ongoing science experiments. Students can visit the center, make observations, take measurements, and log the information.

A Listening Center

Use earphones and a tape player or computer to create an interactive listening and practice center. Provide some kind of response form to be completed when the lesson is completed.

Another approach to centers is to develop them to address language arts or mathematics skills. Tubs and trays, hanging folders, shoeboxes, and file folders are good choices for storage. Portable centers, stored in a central location, lend themselves beautifully to practicing specific skills. Students can take the centers to desks and work areas to complete the activities.

Everything you need for four specific skill centers is provided on pages 176–237. Centers have adaptations for primary and intermediate levels.

Tub or Tray Center—
A Learner Layer Book
pages 176-187

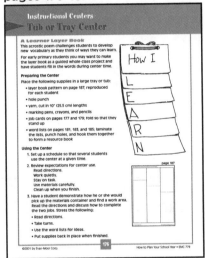

This center may also be set up as a writing center project.

Folder Center—
The Frog Pond
pages 188-205

Shoebox Center—
Just Driving By!
pages 206-221

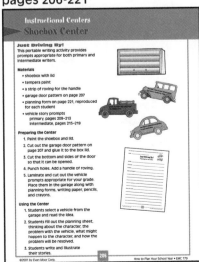

Cross-Legged Critter Center—
Out of this World
pages 222-237

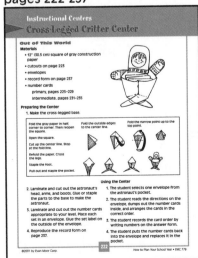

A Learner Layer Book

This acrostic poem challenges students to develop new vocabulary as they think of ways they can learn.

For early primary students you may want to make the layer book as a guided whole-class project and have students fill in the words during center time.

Preparing the Center

Place the following supplies in a large tray or tub:

- layer book pattern on page 187, reproduced for each student

- hole punch

- yarn, cut in 10" (25.5 cm) lengths

- marking pens, crayons, and pencils

- job cards on pages 177 and 179; fold so that they stand up

- word lists on pages 181, 183, and 185; laminate the lists, punch holes, and hook them together to form a resource book

Using the Center

1. Set up a schedule so that several students use the center at a given time.

2. Review expectations for center use.
   Read directions.
   Work quietly.
   Stay on task.
   Use materials carefully.
   Clean up when you finish.

3. Have a student demonstrate how he or she would pick up the materials container and find a work area. Read the directions and discuss how to complete the two jobs. Stress the following:

   - Read directions.

   - Take turns.

   - Use the word lists for ideas.

   - Put supplies back in place when finished.

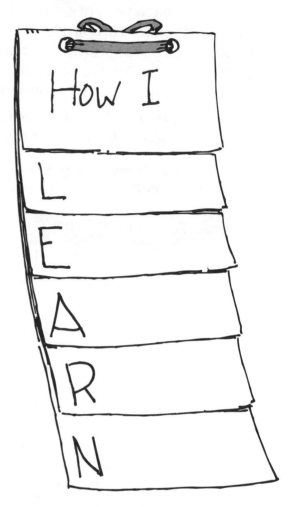

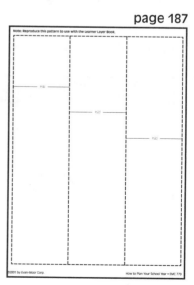

page 187

176

fold

Job 1

Make the Layer Book

1. Cut out the pages of the layer book pattern.

2. Fold on the fold lines.

3. Nest the pages together so that each page is longer than the one before.

4. Punch holes in the fold. Thread a piece of yarn through the holes and tie it to hold the pages together.

How to Plan Your School Year • EMC 779

fold

Job 2

Write the Book

1. On the top flap, write "How I."

2. Write one letter on each of the five other flaps—L-E-A-R-N.

3. Write and/or draw to list ways of learning that begin with the letter on each flap. Use the word lists for ideas.

L

Listen

Look

Live

Labor

Label

Launch

Lead

Locate

Log

E

Edit

Elaborate

Equate

Establish

Examine

Exercise

Expand

Extend

How to Plan Your School Year • EMC 779

A

Answer

Analyze

Anticipate

Ask

Absorb

Access

Argue

R

Review

Read

Reason

Rate

Recite

Receive

Recognize

Record

Redo

How to Plan Your School Year • EMC 779

N

Notice

Name

Negotiate

Number

Nose around

Nurture

Learning Words

Use words like these to complete your layer book.

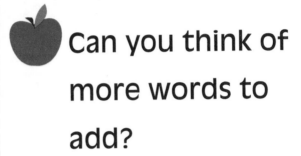 Can you think of more words to add?

Where could you find more words?

How to Plan Your School Year • EMC 779

Note: Reproduce this pattern to use with the Learner Layer Book.

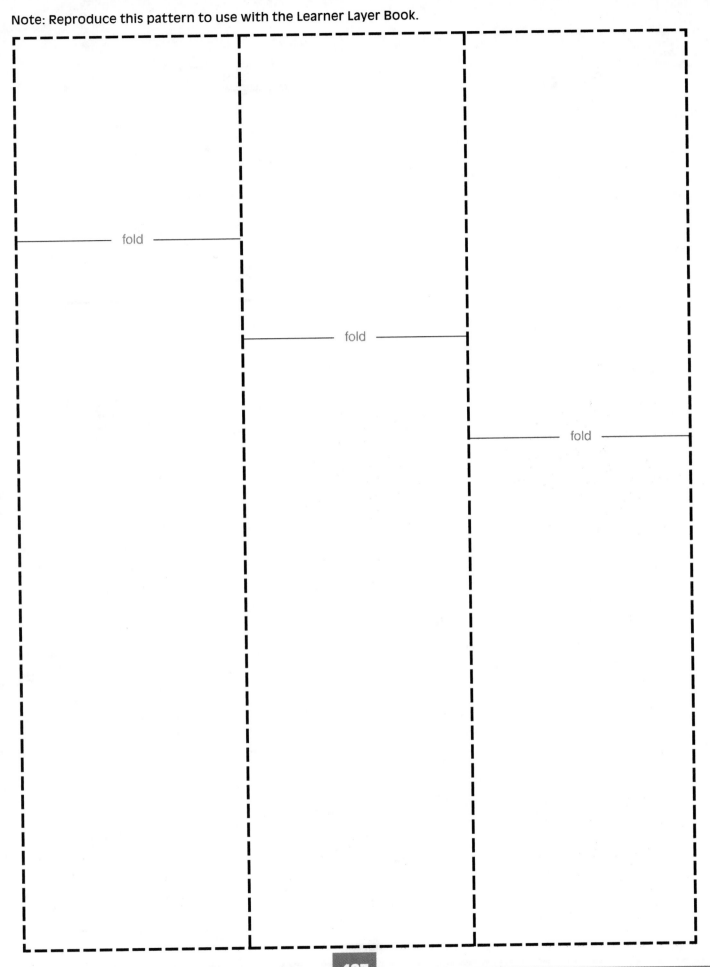

fold

fold

fold

How to Plan Your School Year • EMC 779

The Frog Pond

A colored two-pocket folder holds all the materials needed for this center. Primary students will sort words with short and long vowels. Intermediate students will group synonyms together.

Materials

- folder with two inside pockets
- folder cover on page 189
- record form on page 205, reproduced for each student
- 2 envelopes
- primary—lily pads on page 191
  sorting frogs on pages 193–199
- intermediate—sorting frogs on pages 201 and 203

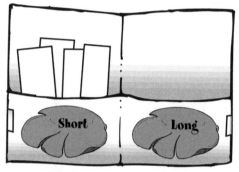

Preparing the Center

1. Laminate and cut out the Frog Pond cover. Glue it to the front of the folder. If the folder pockets are open on the sides, tape them closed.

2. Laminate and cut out the sorting frogs.

3. Place the sorting frogs in envelopes. Frogs of the same color should go together.

   Note: The long vowel words are more difficult.

4. Place the envelopes, record forms, and sorting pads (if used) in the folder pockets. Have a dictionary available for intermediate students.

Using the Center

- **Primary**
  Students take an envelope of cards from the folder. Using the two lily pad sorting boards, the students sort the cards into short and long vowels. List the words on the record form.

- **Intermediate**
  Students take an envelope of cards from the folder. Students sort the word cards into sets of two or three words that are synonyms. List the groups of words on the record form.

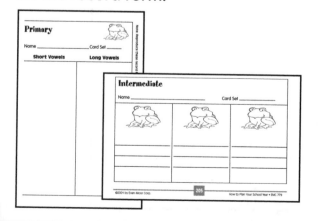

The Frog Pond

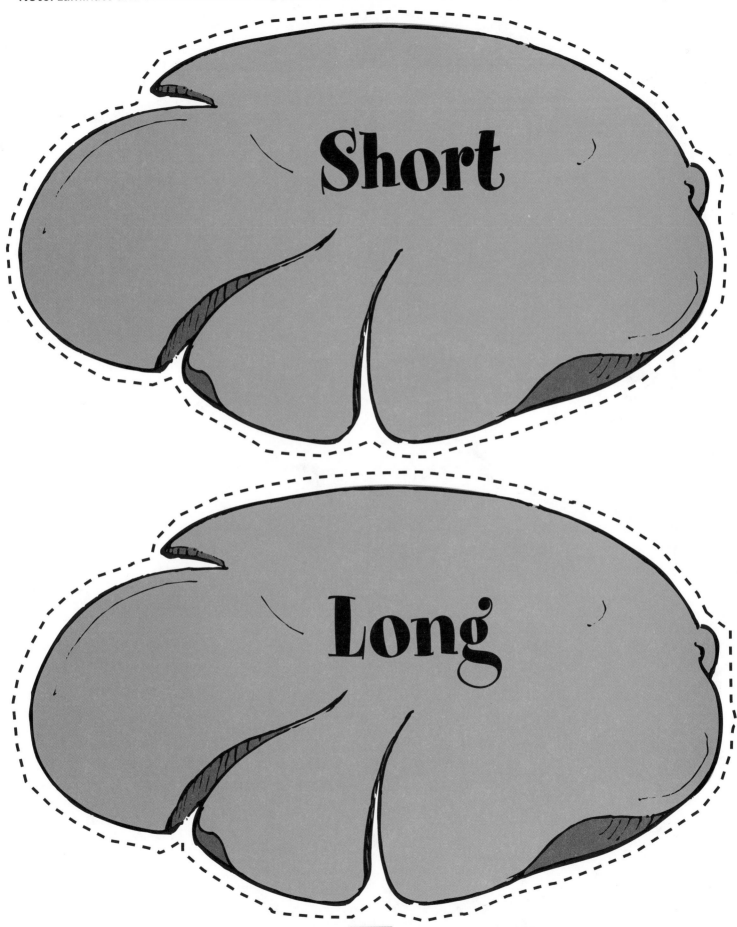

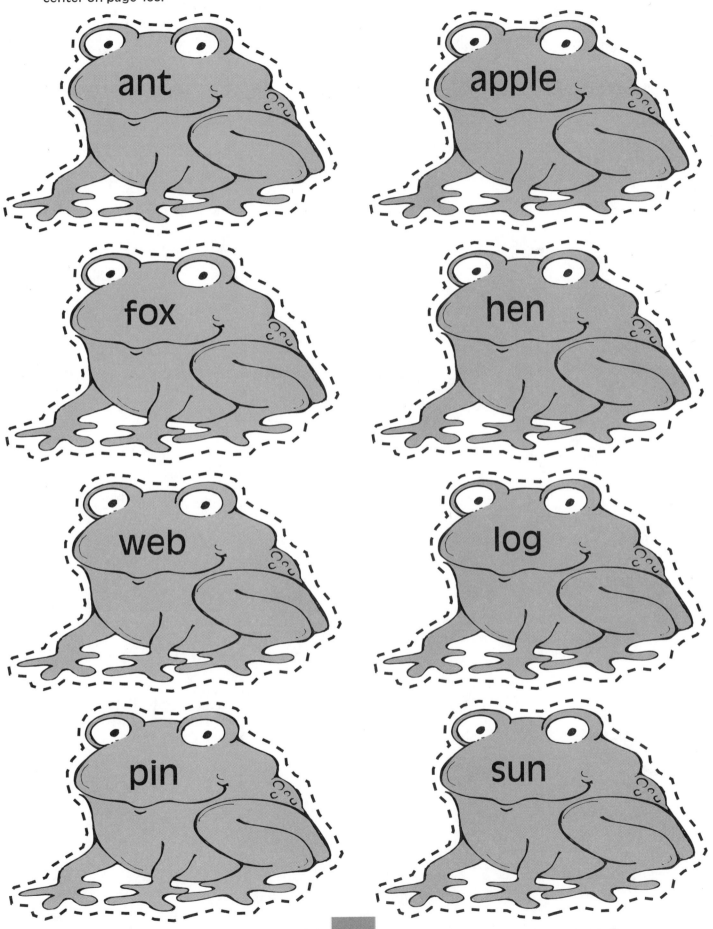

ant

apple

fox

hen

web

log

pin

sun

coat

nose

use

tree

bike

pie

train

cake

flag

little

letter

truck

stand

under

beg

pond

How to Plan Your School Year • EMC 779

Note: Laminate and cut out these sorting frogs for short and long vowel practice using The Frog Pond folder center on page 188.

grapes

leaf

high

fuse

cube

they

speak

snow

199

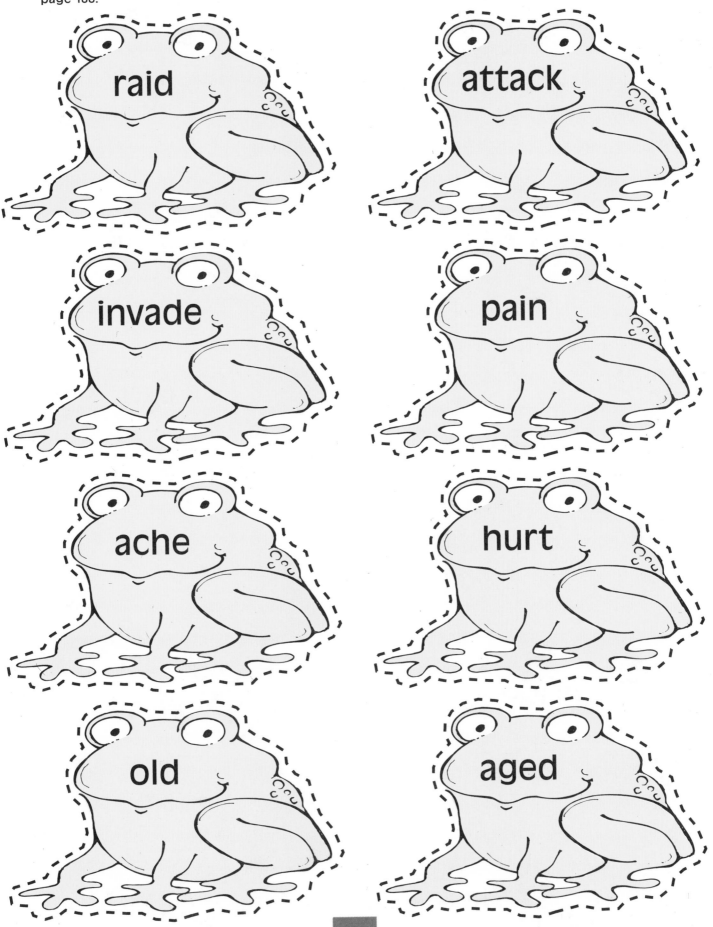

raid

attack

invade

pain

ache

hurt

old

aged

How to Plan Your School Year • EMC 779

Note: Laminate and cut out these sorting frogs for synonym practice using The Frog Pond folder center on page 188.

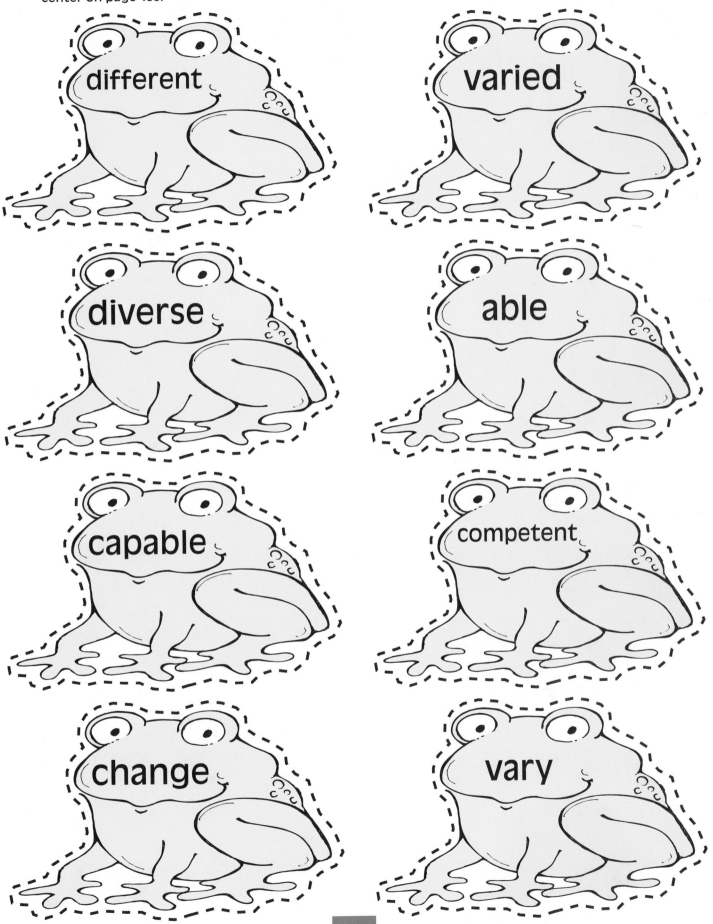

different

varied

diverse

able

capable

competent

change

vary

How to Plan Your School Year • EMC 779

Primary

Name _____

Card Set _____

Long Vowels

Short Vowels

Intermediate

Name _____   Card Set _____

Note: Reproduce these record forms to use with The Frog Pond folder center on page 188.

How to Plan Your School Year • EMC 779

Just Driving By!

This portable writing activity provides prompts appropriate for both primary and intermediate writers.

Materials

- shoebox with lid
- tempera paint
- a strip of roving for the handle
- garage door pattern on page 207
- planning form on page 221, reproduced for each student
- vehicle story prompts
  primary, pages 209–213
  intermediate, pages 215–219

Preparing the Center

1. Paint the shoebox and lid.

2. Cut out the garage door pattern on page 207 and glue it to the box lid.

3. Cut the bottom and sides of the door so that it can be opened.

4. Punch holes. Add a handle of roving.

5. Laminate and cut out the vehicle prompts appropriate for your grade. Place them in the garage along with planning forms, writing paper, pencils, and crayons.

Using the Center

1. Students select a vehicle from the garage and read the idea.

2. Students fill out the planning sheet, thinking about the character, the problem with the vehicle, what might happen to the character, and how the problem will be resolved.

3. Students write and illustrate their stories.

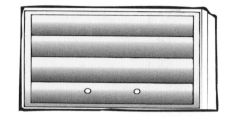

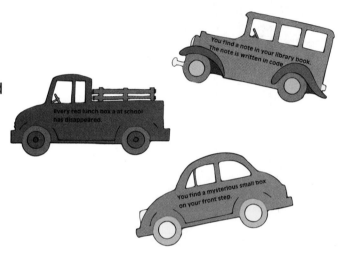

206

Garage Door

1. Cut out the pattern.
2. Glue to a shoebox top.

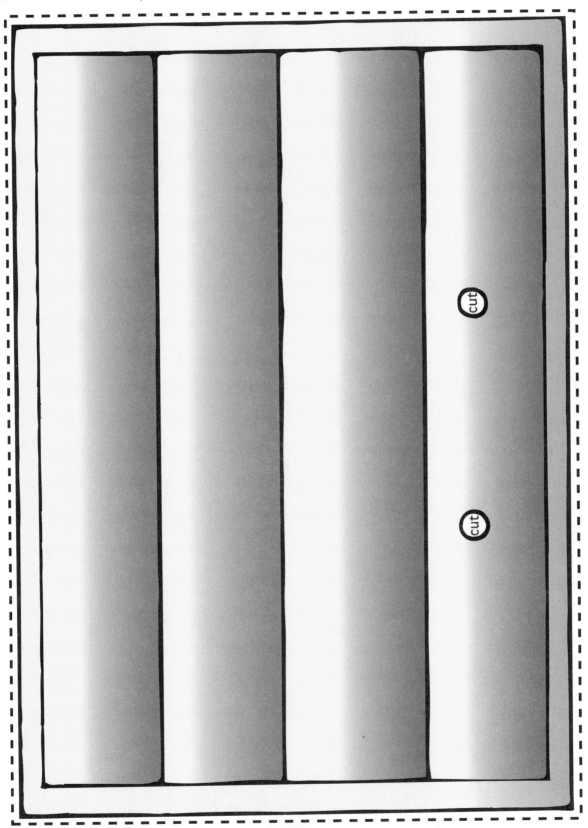

How to Plan Your School Year • EMC 779

Descriptive Writing

A sleek silver limo gets stuck in the mud

A tired tractor faces a huge task

A nifty new jeep is sitting in your driveway

209

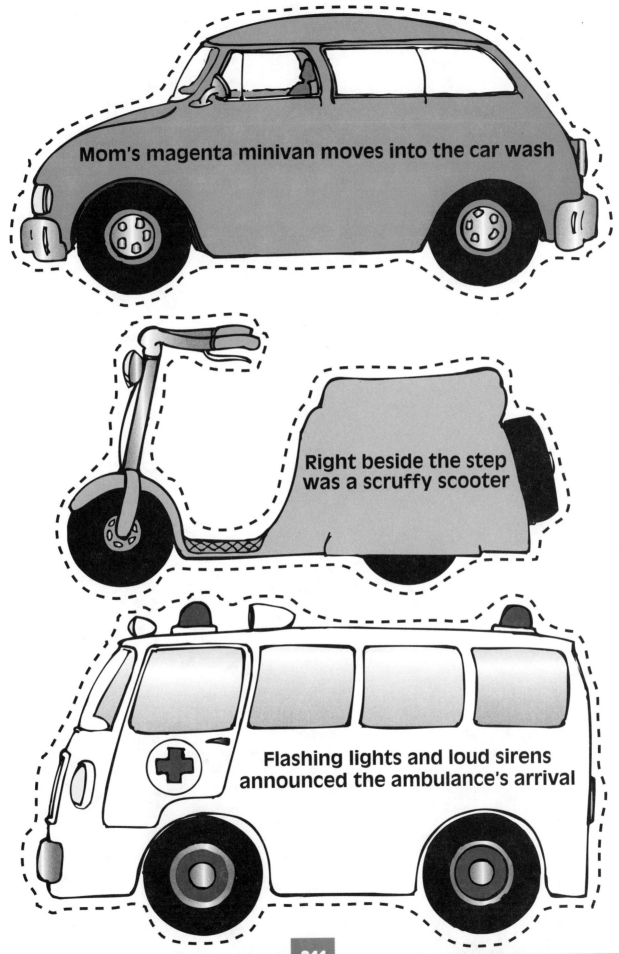

Mom's magenta minivan moves into the car wash

Right beside the step was a scruffy scooter

Flashing lights and loud sirens announced the ambulance's arrival

How to Plan Your School Year • EMC 779

Your trusty mountain bike has a flat tire

A pink pickup pulls out of the parking lot

A mighty motorcycle roars by

Note: Laminate and cut out these vehicle story prompts to use with the Just Driving By! shoebox center on page 206.

Mystery Writing

You find an old coat on the seat of your car. When you look in the pocket, you find...?

You see a note on your desk when you get to school. It says "Watch this spot."

The girl looked in the rearview mirror and saw that her face was blue.

You find a note in your library book. The note is written in code.

Every red lunch box at school has disappeared.

You find a mysterious small box on your front step.

How to Plan Your School Year • EMC 779

Your dog refuses to go inside the doghouse.

The bus leaves for school before you get to the corner, but when you get to school it hasn't arrived.

A caravan of purple police cars speed past your house.

Name: _____

Just Driving By!

Planning for Your Story

Vehicle: _____

Character: _____

Problem: _____

What will happen? _____

_____

_____

_____

_____

How will it end? _____

_____

_____

_____

_____

How to Plan Your School Year • EMC 779

Cross-Legged Critter Center

Out of This World

Materials

- 12" (30.5 cm) square of gray construction paper
- cutouts on page 223
- envelopes
- record form on page 237
- number cards

    primary, pages 225–229

    intermediate, pages 231–235

Preparing the Center

1. Make the cross-legged base.

a. Fold the gray paper in half, corner to corner. Then reopen the square.

b. Fold the outside edges to the center line.

d. Open the square.

c. Fold the narrow point up to the top point.

e. Cut up the center line. Stop at the fold line.

f. Refold the paper. Cross the legs.

g. Staple the foot.

h. Pull out and staple the pocket.

2. Laminate and cut out the astronaut's head, arms, and boots. Glue or staple the parts to the base to make the astronaut.

3. Laminate and cut out the number cards appropriate to your level. Place each set in an envelope. Glue the set label on the outside of the envelope.

4. Reproduce the record form on page 237.

Using the Center

1. The student selects one envelope from the astronaut's pocket.

2. The student reads the directions on the envelope, dumps out the number cards inside, and arranges the cards in the correct order.

3. The student records the card order by writing numbers on the answer form.

4. The student puts the number cards back into the envelope and replaces it in the pocket.

How to Plan Your School Year • EMC 779

Note: Laminate and cut out these cutouts to complete the Astronaut for the Out of This World center on page 222.

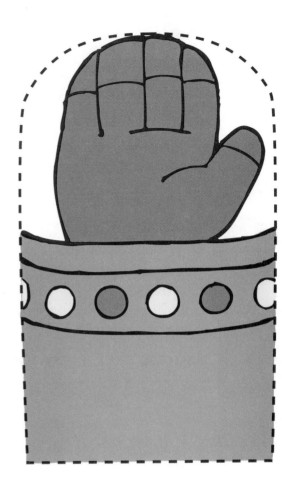

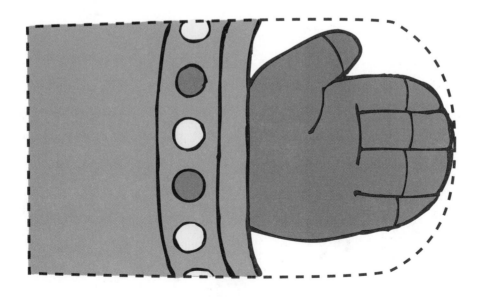

Counting by 5s

Card Set 1

Put the cards in order to show skip-counting by 5s.

0	5	10	15	20
25	30	35	40	45
50	55	60	65	70
75	80	85	90	95
100	105	110	115	120

How to Plan Your School Year • EMC 779

Card Set 2

Counting by 10s

Put the cards in order to show skip-counting by 10s.

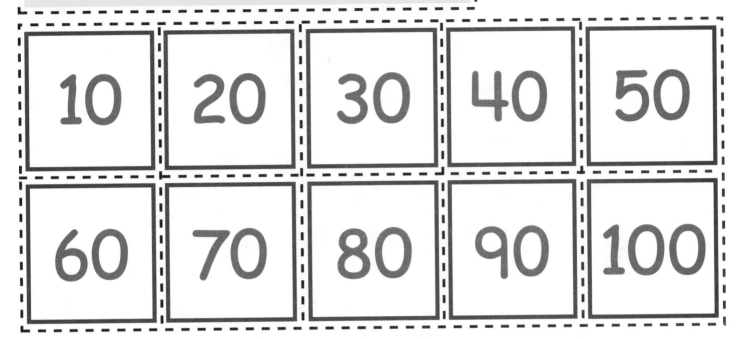

Card Set 3

Counting by 2s

Put the cards in order to show skip-counting by 2s.

How to Plan Your School Year • EMC 779

Card Set 4

Counting by 3s

Put the cards in order to show skip-counting by 3s.

3	6	9	12	15
18	21	24	27	30

Card Set 5

Counting by 4s

Put the cards in order to show skip-counting by 4s.

4	8	12	16	20
24	28	32	36	40

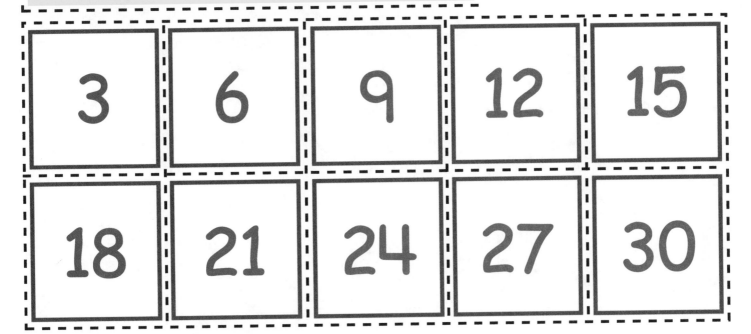

How to Plan Your School Year • EMC 779

Card Set 1

Decimals

Put these cards in order from smallest to largest.

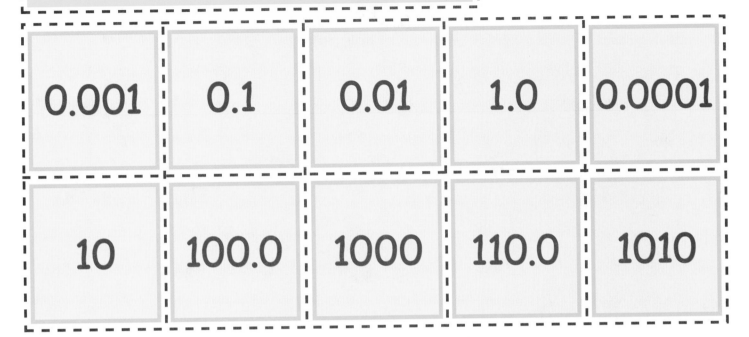

| 0.001 | 0.1 | 0.01 | 1.0 | 0.0001 |
| 10 | 100.0 | 1000 | 110.0 | 1010 |

Card Set 2

Fractions

Put these cards in order from smallest to largest.

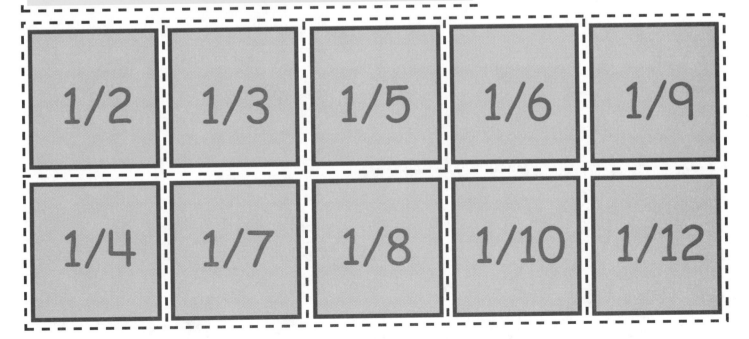

| 1/2 | 1/3 | 1/5 | 1/6 | 1/9 |
| 1/4 | 1/7 | 1/8 | 1/10 | 1/12 |

How to Plan Your School Year • EMC 779

Card Set 3

Decimals

Put these cards in order from smallest to largest.

| 5.9 | 9.5 | 0.59 | 9.59 | 95.9 |
| 59 | 5.95 | 59.5 | 959 | 0.959 |

Card Set 4

Fractions

Put these cards in order from smallest to largest.

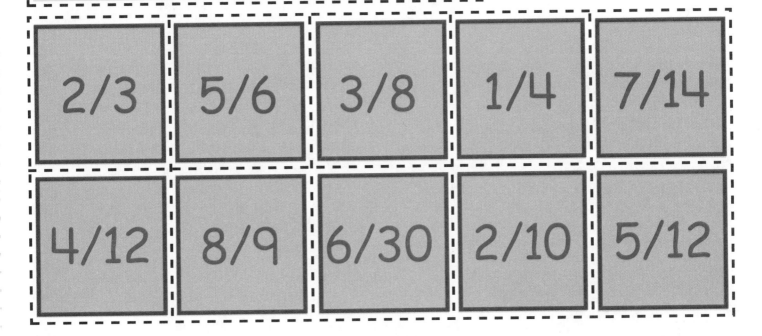

| 2/3 | 5/6 | 3/8 | 1/4 | 7/14 |
| 4/12 | 8/9 | 6/30 | 2/10 | 5/12 |

How to Plan Your School Year • EMC 779

Card Set 5

Decimals

Put these cards in order from smallest to largest.

| 23.1 | 321 | 21.3 | 0.321 | 13.2 |
| 1.23 | 2.13 | 123 | 3.21 | 32.1 |

Card Set 6

Fractions

Put these cards in order from smallest to largest.

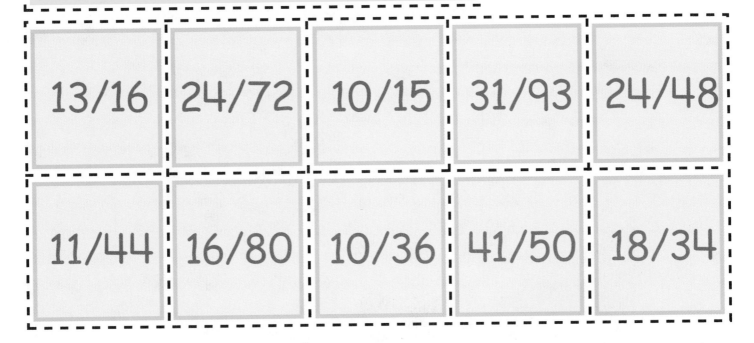

| 13/16 | 24/72 | 10/15 | 31/93 | 24/48 |
| 11/44 | 16/80 | 10/36 | 41/50 | 18/34 |

How to Plan Your School Year • EMC 779

Note: Reproduce this record form to be used with the Out of This World center on page 222.

Card Set

Name: ________________

Out of This World

Record Form

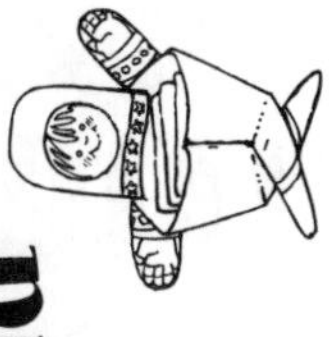

Card Set

Name: ________________

Out of This World

Record Form

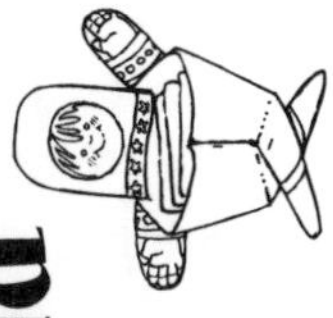

Cooperative Learning

■ Cooperative learning techniques will help you organize your instruction.

■ The basic goal of cooperative learning is to have students work as a team to learn something.

This section includes suggestions for forming cooperative learning teams, a review of cooperative learning techniques, as well as sample cooperative activities.

Contents

Creating Teams of Four Students

The key element to cooperative learning is the **team.** Here's how to form teams:

- If the total number of students in your class is not divisible by four, make a team or two of five students. When you make a team of fewer than four or more than five students, you lose important dynamics.

- Teams should be of mixed gender, abilities, and ethnicity.

- Identify partner pairs within each team, carefully pairing a student at a higher academic level with a student at a lower level.

- Group desks so that the four teammates sit closely together.

- Keep the same teams for at least four weeks at a time.

- Encourage teammates to create a team identity. They might choose a team name, make a poster or placard, write a slogan, or design a flag.

- After forming new teams, engage students in a team-building activity.

A Cooperative Learning Lesson Format

Any kind of lesson can be formatted to facilitate cooperative learning.

- Information is presented.

  Students sit in teams. Begin the lesson by presenting information to the whole class, using an interactive method. Ask questions and allow teams to brainstorm before you give specific information. Give students an activity to demonstrate the concept you are about to explain. Ask for feedback relating the concepts to their personal experiences.

- Teammates practice.

  Give several practice problems or discussion questions related to the information you have presented. Teammates solve and discuss the problems together. Randomly call on a student from one or two teams and ask, "What answer does your team have?"

- Teammates work together on an activity.

  Give an assignment related to the topic. Teammates work together to help and support each other, but each student is required to produce an individual product that receives an individual grade. For example, the team may analyze a model ship, but each team member completes a labeled diagram of the ship.

- Students are assessed.

  Teammates study and practice together for a test, but they take the test individually for an individual grade.

239

Students won't just naturally work together as a team, but there are techniques you can use to encourage participation.

Recognize Appropriate Behavior

Throughout a lesson, recognize teams for exhibiting appropriate behavior, such as working well together, keeping noise at the correct level, and assisting each other.

- Use verbal praise. Tell them specifically what they did to merit the praise. *Wow! Look at how the Blue Whale team is using 6" voices just as I asked. Excellent job!*

- Award points throughout a lesson for teams displaying appropriate behavior. Total the points at the end of the week for rewards.

  Use a simple method to record the points such as tally marks on the chalkboard, wipe-off boards, or thermometer-like strips marked with numbers—use a clothespin to point to a number. Allow students to keep track of points as much as possible.

Teacher Visits

During every lesson, spend time visiting each team. Praise teams working well together. Be sure to tell them what they are doing well, give suggestions for ways they can cooperate even more, and demonstrate how problems can be solved by working as a team.

Reward Academic Progress

You might reward a team if all members turn in all assignments and homework, or all members reach a certain grade goal on an assignment or test. Remember to take into account individual student ability when setting grade goals. This might mean that each team member has a different grade goal.

Teach About Teamwork

- Occasionally ask a team to model appropriate cooperative learning techniques. Have them show how to help a teammate without actually giving the answer, encourage a teammate, make sure every teammate contributes to a discussion, or divide a task into duties for each teammate.

- Hold occasional discussions about the strengths of working as a team. Use real-world examples of successful teamwork, such as sports teams, architects designing a new building, or detectives trying to solve a case.

Helpful Hint

Co-op Groups

Compliment students on their successful use of specific cooperative strategies before complimenting them on the results of their work.

240

Ask Your Team, Then the Teacher

Studies show that many questions students ask do not require a teacher's response. So train your students to use their teammates as their first resource if they have a question.

- First, they ask their teammates.

- If the question cannot be answered, then they ask you.

  You can emphasize this process by first asking, "Did you ask your team first?" whenever a question is asked.

Silence Signal

Develop a simple signal that you can use to quiet the classroom, such as flicking the lights off and on, clapping twice, or holding up your fingers in the peace symbol. Train students to recognize the signal and immediately stop talking when they see it.

This is an excellent method to lower the noise level in the room or to get silence when you need to speak. It is important that you model the signal correctly by not speaking when using the symbol. Practice the signal often in the beginning until response is habitual.

Ready-Set-Go

Use this method to facilitate movement in your classroom. Instead of students scrambling to line up or leave the room for dismissal, establish the following procedure.

- Say, "Ready."

  Students stop what they are doing, put their materials away, and get backpacks ready. Wait until this is completed.

- Say, "Set."

  Students stand, push in their chairs, and remain quietly behind their chairs. Wait until this is completed.

- Say, "Go."

  Students move at a walk to the required spot.

  This technique is also effective when students are required to get materials in the room.

Mini-Meetings

When teams are working together on an activity, hold mini-meetings with each team for a minute or two each. During this time do the following:

- Make sure students are on task.

- Make sure teammates are helping each other to learn, but are completing individual work as well.

- Reiterate directions and concepts.

- Encourage and praise students.

- Help students experiencing difficulty.

- Collect finished work.

Cooperative Learning Techniques

Think-Pair-Share

Developed by Frank Lyman at the University of Maryland, this technique is one of the best methods of asking a question. It works like this:

- When you have a question during a lesson, ask it to the class and say, "THINK about an answer to this." No hands are raised, no answers are shouted out; students simply sit at their desks and think about the question. Allow them five or six seconds to think.

- Say, "Turn to your partner and give one possible answer to this question." Be sure to tell them specifically what you want them to do with their partner. For example, give one possible answer or come up with two solutions. Allow no more than 20 seconds for this step. That's enough time for each partner in the PAIR to speak, but not enough time to get off task.

- Randomly choose a representative from one or two teams to SHARE a response. You can ask, "What is one answer you or your partner came up with?" It is not necessary to poll every team. If other students seem anxious to contribute, you may say, "Give me a thumbs up if your team had a similar answer."

Think-Pair-Share eliminates the need for students to raise hands or shout out answers, prepares every student to answer, and lets all students know they may be called on to respond.

Letter Heads

Assign a letter (e.g., W, X, Y, Z) to each teammate on every team. Then when you want to randomly choose a student to do the SHARE part of Think-Pair-Share, you can say, "Can Letter Y on the Blue Whale team share one answer?"

This technique keeps your selection random and prevents students from feeling put "on the spot" by having their name called out. You might write the letters on pieces of masking tape and place them on the desks so that students remember their letters.

Use "Letter Heads" to also facilitate student movement. Say, "Will all the Letter W's please come up and get supplies for your team's experiment."

You may use any series of letters, although using A, B, C, and D might make students think of letter grades and have bad connotations for those assigned the C or D!

Around the Table

This is a quick method allowing students to brainstorm. Ask a question, then ask the Letter W person to jot down a response on paper. The Letter W person then passes the paper to Letter X, who also writes a response and passes the paper to Letter Y, and so on. Teams continue passing the paper around to their teammates until time is called, usually after a minute or two. Generally this technique works with questions that require a response of one or two words. For example: "Write down a way that people use division in their everyday lives. Write down a state in the United States. Write down a word starting with Q."

242

Jigsaw

The Jigsaw technique was developed by Elliot Anderson in the 1970s. It breaks down a task into simple parts, requiring teammates to become an expert with their part and to share their knowledge with the rest of the team.

For example, if your class is studying the Vikings, you could use Jigsaw as follows:

- Ask the Letter W persons from all the teams to assemble, go to the media center, and together research the religion of the Vikings. The Letter X's are to use the classroom set of encyclopedias to research the food of the Vikings. The Letter Y's use the Internet to research Viking transportation. The Letter Z's listen to the teacher give a talk about Viking history. Each of these groups are considered expert groups. The expert groups have a representative from each team. Together they become experts on their topic.

- When the expert groups complete their research, students return to their home teams. Now each team has one expert in each Viking topic—religion, food, transportation, and history.

- Each individual presents expert information to the team. The Letter W person discusses Viking religion as the other teammates listen and take notes. Then the Letter X person talks about Viking food, and so on.

Jigsaw allows a complex task (such as learning about Viking culture) to be broken down into parts and accomplished more quickly. Individual students are responsible for becoming an expert on a topic, presenting the information to their team, and then listening to others share their expertise.

Helpful Hint

Call the cooperative learning technique by name. "Make a community circle in the library area." Your students will move quickly into place and know what to expect.

243

Sometimes teachers resist cooperative learning because they are afraid of noisy classrooms or losing control of their students. A well-run cooperative learning classroom can be a teacher's dream. Instead of dealing with 30 individual students, a teacher can focus on seven teams of students who function as a cohesive unit.

Keep in mind, though, that it takes a concerted effort on the teacher's part to make cooperative learning work well. Have a plan in place to deal with problems that may occur. The following trouble-shooting chart can help solve problems. Use your creativity and positive attitude to personalize it for your classroom.

Problem:

One student does no work on the team.

Possible Solutions:

- Pull the student aside and discuss the importance of teamwork, and why every member is valuable to the success of the team.

- Relate the student's participation to the team reward. "Your team is so close to getting 50 points and a prize...if you participate today it's sure to happen."

- Pull the student from the team to work alone for a day. Usually they miss the camaraderie and want to rejoin the team.

Important: Avoid reassigning students to other teams. Doing this sets a bad precedent. It says that if you don't like your team, you can move by not doing any work. Students must learn to work together, even if it is with individuals that aren't necessarily their friends.

Problem:

Teams are noisy when they work together.

Possible Solutions:

- Establish the noise level for every activity and model it as needed.

- Use your silence signal to remind students of the appropriate noise level.

- As teams work together, move throughout the room to monitor the noise.

Problem:

One student does all the work for the team.

Possible Solutions:

• Make each student responsible for a written response to the assignment.

• Use the Jigsaw strategy that requires participation from all team members.

• As teams work together, move throughout the room to monitor what each student is doing, and to stress participation by all team members.

Problem:

One team member is absent often.

Possible Solutions:

• Make that person the fifth member of a team so that even when he or she is absent, the team can function with the four remaining students.

• Talk to the parents to see why the student is absent so often.

Problem:

The teacher cannot visit every team for a mini-meeting each day.

Possible Solutions:

• Divide your available time by the number of teams to get a rough idea of the amount of time you can spend with each team. If you have about 20 minutes to do mini-meetings as your six teams work on an activity, you can spend about 3 minutes with each team.

• Concentrate on teams/students who need the most assistance.

• Keep a checklist of tasks you want to accomplish with each team during mini-meetings.

Problem:

Teammates argue or fight.

Possible Solutions:

• Relate their behavior to the reward system you have established. "Remember, I'm awarding 10 points to teams who are using the 6" voice during this activity."

• Ignore teams who are behaving inappropriately and instead praise teams that are on task.

• If using a point reward system, do not award points to a team that misbehaves. Do not take away points they have already earned.

• Use Around the Table to get responses.

In the Circle

Students use a Venn diagram to respond to questions asked by the teacher.

Materials (per team)

- posterboard or large piece of paper
- markers

Time Allowance

10–30 minutes

Advance Preparation

None

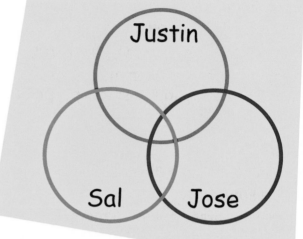

Directions

1. Divide the class into teams of three students.

2. Give each team a piece of posterboard or a large piece of paper.

3. Have them draw three large intersecting circles. Each writes his or her name in one circle.

4. One at a time, ask the teams five to ten questions. Team members will respond within their teams. They record responses by writing or drawing inside the appropriate areas. Allow time for all team members to respond before asking the next question.

Examples of questions you can ask include:

What is your favorite _____?

food	animal	cartoon	vegetable
movie	cereal	restaurant	brand of gym shoe
computer game	book	time to get up	number
singing group	time to go to bed	school subject	TV star

Variation

Tailor your list to relate to the theme or subject your class will study. For example, if the topic is the five senses, the list might include favorite smells, tastes, sights, sounds, and touches. If the topic is literature, the list could include favorite authors, books, illustrators, and subjects.

Freaky Fairy Tales

Students draw cards naming fairy tale characters and settings. The group must create a story using all those elements.

Materials

- character and setting cards on pages 248–250, reproduced for each team
- story planner on page 251, reproduced for each team
- small bags
- paper and pencils

Time Allowance

60 minutes

Advance Preparation

Reproduce two or three copies of the story cards. Cut them apart and put four or five cards into a bag for each group. Make sure there is a mixture of character and setting cards.

Directions

1. Divide the class into teams of four or five.

2. Give a bag to each team, and ask each team member to choose one card.

3. Instruct each group to create a freaky fairy tale using the characters and settings they chose. Stories may be written or oral. Teams use the story planner to outline the story they develop together. If students can write, allow them to fill in the organizer, otherwise they can simply discuss each element.

4. Teams present their stories to the class. Illustrations may be added as well.

5. Create a class booklet that includes all the stories.

Character Cards

Character	Character
Little Red Riding Hood	The Big Bad Wolf
Jack in the Beanstalk	Baby Bear from Goldilocks
One of the Three Little Pigs	Fairy Godmother from Cinderella
Grumpy	Little Red Hen

Character	Character
Popeye	Pinnochio
Prince Charming	Humpty Dumpty
The Frog Prince	Cinderella
Thumbelina	The Big Bad Wolf

Setting Cards

Setting	Setting
A castle	Grandmothers House
The White House	A house made of straw

Fairy Tale Story Planner

Team Name: _____

Characters
Who is in the story? _____

Setting
Where does the story happen? When does it happen? _____

Plot
What happens? _____

How to Plan Your School Year • EMC 779

Note: Reproduce these cards to use with Freaky Fairy Tales on page 247.

Character Cards

Character Little Red Riding Hood	**Character** The Big Bad Wolf
Character Jack in the Beanstalk	**Character** Baby Bear from Goldilocks
Character One of the Three Little Pigs	**Character** Fairy Godmother from Cinderella
Character Grumpy	**Character** Little Red Hen

Note: Reproduce these cards to use with Freaky Fairy Tales on page 247.

Character Cards

Character Popeye	**Character** Pinnochio
Character Prince Charming	**Character** Humpty Dumpty
Character The Frog Prince	**Character** Cinderella
Character Thumbelina	**Character** The Big Bad Wolf

Note: Reproduce these cards to use with Freaky Fairy Tales on page 247.

Setting Cards

Setting A castle	**Setting** Grandmother's house
Setting The White House	**Setting** A house made of straw
Setting A ballroom	**Setting** The home of the Three Bears
Setting The mall	**Setting** A gingerbread house

Fairy Tale Story Planner

Team Name _____

Characters
Who is in the story? _____

Setting
Where does the story happen? When does it happen? _____

_____

Plot
What happens? _____

_____

Fairy Tale Story Planner

Team Name _____

Characters
Who is in the story? _____

Setting
Where does the story happen? When does it happen? _____

_____

Plot
What happens? _____

_____

How to Plan Your School Year • EMC 779

Newspaper Scavenger Hunt

Materials (per team)

- complete newspaper (Each team should have the same newspaper.)
- 4 to 5 pairs of scissors
- glue or gluestick
- 12" x 18" (30.5 x 45.5 cm) posterboard
- scavenger hunt list (page 254)

Time Allowance

15–30 minutes

Advance Preparation

1. Gather a copy of the same newspaper for each team.
2. Create a scavenger hunt list of items teams must find in the newspaper. Write the list on the form on page 254. Consider the time available and the level of the students to determine how long or how complex the list should be. Items may be simple or complex, depending on the grade level.
3. Reproduce the list for each team.

Directions

1. Give each team a complete newspaper and a scavenger hunt list.
2. Set a time limit.
3. Explain that teams are to find as many of the items on the list as they can, cut them out, and glue them to the posterboard in the order they are listed.

Possible Scavenger Hunt Items

- a baby
- sports equipment
- a picture of a politician
- an animal
- a tie score from a game
- a country in Europe
- a word with 10 or more letters
- a children's movie
- a metric measurement
- something scary
- a picture of the president
- an ethnic restaurant
- somebody who isn't smiling
- a food item on sale
- a five-syllable word

Variations

The items you choose for the list may relate to the course of study that you are about to begin. For example, if you are studying the environment, the list might include items about recycling, pollution, and graphs related to trash. Instead of newspapers, use old magazines, catalogs, or sales fliers for the hunt.

A Towering Achievement

This activity is a good way to begin lessons on architecture, cities, skyscrapers, gravity, geometry, or measurement.

Materials (per team)

- 10 straws
- 10 paper clips
- 4 sheets of paper
- pair of scissors

Time Allowance

15–25 minutes

Advance Preparation

Assemble the materials listed for each team.

Directions

1. Give the materials to each team. Their goal is to build the highest tower.

2. Each team gets 5 minutes to discuss its plan and 10 to 20 minutes to build a tower following these rules:

   - The tower must be freestanding. It can't rest against anything.

   - It can lean as long as it doesn't touch anything. (Think Pisa!)

   - Only the materials supplied may be used. If a mistake is made in cutting, team members have to live with it.

Variation

Depending on the grade level, you may add additional materials to the list to provide for more complex solutions—card stock, tape, or toothpicks, for example.

253

Scavenger Hunt List

Teamwork

I am one and only one,
What little can I do?
But if I get a friend to join
Together we are two.

If each of us gets one more friend--
Together we are four,
And working side by side by side
We can do so much more.

So it goes, our numbers grow.
Our confidence grows, too.
When we join to work together
There's nothing we can't do.

©John Micklos, Jr.

Parent Communication

- Parents are a vital part of each child's education team.

- It is important to establish a good connection with parents.

- Share your goals and expectations and your discipline plan with parents.

This section includes forms and certificates to make parent communication easy.

Contents

How will you communicate with parents this year? Use a variety of resources. Just as you have established routines with your students, establish routines with parents.

- Send home a folder of work and the class newsletter every Friday and have students return the folder with a parent's signature and comments on Monday.

- Send postcards with positive anecdotal comments.

- Make monthly or quarterly phone calls to track progress.

- Hold Parent/Student/Teacher conferences several times a year.

- Plan special events for the year: Back to School Night, Reading Party, Family Math or Science Nights, Class Plays or Performances, Volunteer Thank-you Teas.

On the following pages you will find some reproducible forms that will help you establish and maintain good parent communication.

Newsletter Forms
pages 259-262

Notes and Awards
pages 263-269

Parentgram
page 270

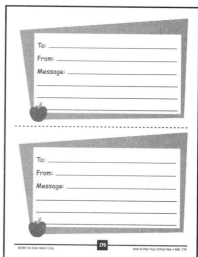

Fall News

from room _____

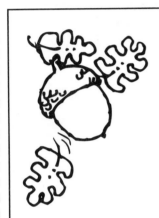

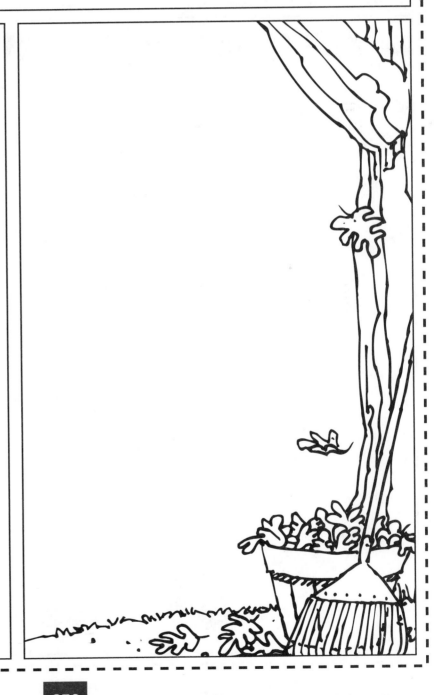

Winter Wonders

from room _____

Coming Soon

What We Did

How to Plan Your School Year • EMC 779

Springing from

room _____

Summer Highlights

from room _____

I had a great day!

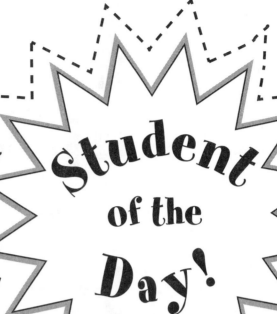

Student of the Day!

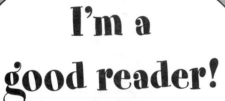

I'm a good reader!

Teacher Helper

Just for you

A+
Excellent!

Just for you

WOW!

Just for you

SUPER
HELPER!

Just for you

Cooperation
is the key

Just for you

YOU
can do it!

Just for you

Great
work!

How to Plan Your School Year • EMC 779

Just for you

BRAVO

Just for you

Congratulations!

Just for you

Terrific

Just for you

YAY!

Just for you

Super Job!

Just for you

YOU can do it

Super Work!

Name

For

Date

How to Plan Your School Year • EMC 779

What a Great Sport!

_____
Name

_____
Date

SPECIAL
Award

_____
Name

_____
For

_____
Date

How to Plan Your School Year • EMC 779

Star Listener

_____
name

_____
date

How to Plan Your School Year • EMC 779

To: _____

From: _____

Message: _____

_____

_____

_____

- -

To: _____

From: _____

Message: _____

_____

_____

_____

Planning for a Substitute

■ There are times when you will have to have a substitute.

■ Planning ahead will enable you to feel relaxed about being out of the classroom.

■ Prepare a Substitute Folder that includes the important information your substitute will need.

This section includes substitute plans for a theme-based day for both a primary and an intermediate classroom.

Contents

With your class develop expectations for their behavior with a substitute. Let them know that you will be in communication with the sub. You expect the substitute to do a good job and you expect your class to do a good job.

Facilitate planning by preparing a substitute folder.

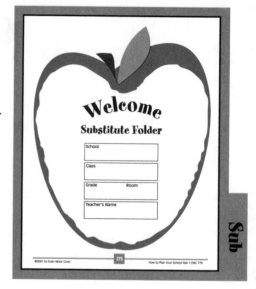

1. Cut out and laminate the sub folder cover on page 273.

2. Staple it to a pocket folder.

3. Reproduce and fill in the substitute forms on pages 275–285.

4. Place the forms in the folder. Be sure to include:

    • a class list with transportation information

    • a basic schedule or an alternative sub schedule

    • opening, attendance, lunch, and dismissal routines. Write out step-by-step directions for each.

    • a set of name tags for your students

    • a list of students who attend special classes and the schedule for these classes

    • a copy of the fire drill and other emergency procedures

When an emergency occurs and you don't have time to plan, you can be ready if you have run off the alternative sub plans found in this section. There is one plan for a primary day and one for an intermediate day. Each is a theme-based day with practice in reading, writing, and math.

Helpful Hint

Have a substitute folder ready when school begins. You never know when you might need it. There is nothing worse than getting sick and THEN having to write substitute plans.

Welcome

Substitute Folder

School

Class

Grade   Room

Teacher's Name

Important People to Know at School

Name: _____

Location: _____

Principal: _____

School Secretary: _____

School Nurse: _____

Librarian: _____

Classroom Assistant: _____

Other Teachers at
This Grade Level: _____

_____

_____

_____

Ask These People
If You Need Help: _____

_____

_____

Custodian: _____

Other: _____

How to Plan Your School Year • EMC 779

A a B b C c D d E e F f G g H h I i J j K k L l M m N n

______________ School's Daily Schedule

Class Begins ______________

Morning Recess ______________

Lunch ______________

Afternoon Recess ______________

Dismissal ______________

Lunch Count Procedures ______________

____

____

____

____

School Bus Information ______________

____

____

____

Special Procedures

What to do if a parent wants to pick up a child directly from class:

_____

_____

How to reach the school nurse or office for assistance:

_____

_____

In case of student illness:

_____

_____

Fire drill procedure:

(See school map for route.)

_____

_____

_____

Other emergency drills:

_____

_____

_____

_____

Students with special health conditions:

_____

_____

_____

_____

Seating Chart

Class List

Discipline Plan

General Philosophy

_____

_____

_____

_____

_____

_____

Classroom Rules

_____

_____

_____

_____

Other School Rules

_____

_____

_____

_____

Discipline Plan

Discipline Techniques

_____

_____

_____

_____

_____

Consequences

_____

_____

_____

Reinforcements and Rewards

_____

_____

_____

How to Plan Your School Year • EMC 779

Special Teachers

The following students receive assistance from specialist teachers.

Time	Student Name	Specialist's Name and Title	Location
_____	_____	_____	_____
_____	_____	_____	_____
_____	_____	_____	_____
_____	_____	_____	_____
_____	_____	_____	_____
_____	_____	_____	_____
_____	_____	_____	_____
_____	_____	_____	_____
_____	_____	_____	_____
_____	_____	_____	_____

Special Duties

Before School

_____

_____

_____

Recess

_____

_____

_____

Lunch

_____

_____

_____

After School

_____

_____

_____

Where to Find It!

Books

- textbooks _____

- other _____

Supplies

- writing paper _____

- pencils _____

- crayons, etc. _____

- construction paper _____

- paste and glue _____

- hand towels _____

P.E. Equipment

- balls _____

- ropes _____

How to Plan Your School Year • EMC 779

Map of the School

Substitute Response Form

Day's Evaluation

I'd rate this day a

1	2	3	4	5	6	7	8	9	10

really
tough

an absolute
delight

These things went well: _____

_____

_____

We had a/some problems with... _____

_____

_____

It would have helped me if... _____

_____

_____

Things that require your attention: _____

_____

_____

I'd also like to say... _____

_____

_____

_____

How to Plan Your School Year • EMC 779

General Directions

Pages 287–294 contain substitute plans for a primary classroom based on the theme of "Ants."

- Reproduce the lesson plan on page 287. Indicate the time period when each activity should be conducted.

- Reproduce the student pages detailed below.

- File the plans in your sub folder. In an emergency, your sub plans will be ready.

- Leave additional resources such as fiction and nonfiction books on ants, with follow-up suggestions that may be used if further activities are needed.

Plan Specifics

Reading

An Ant's Voice
Reproduce the story on pages 288 and 289, the comprehension activity on page 290, and the vocabulary worksheet on page 291.

Writing

Supply writing and drawing paper.

Music and Fun

- Reproduce the song and puppet pattern on page 292.

- Provide craft sticks, crayons or marking pens, and glue to make the stick puppets.

Math

- Reproduce the ant manipulatives on page 293.

- Provide writing paper, scissors, and crayons.

Science

Make a transparency of page 294 and reproduce the page for individual students.

Dear Substitute,

Here are lesson plans to use in my absence. The theme for these fun activities is **Ants, Ants, Ants**. All the student activity pages have been reproduced and are included in this folder. Thank you.

Reading—*An Ant's Voice* | Time: |

• Read this folktale.

• Complete the comprehension and vocabulary worksheets.

Writing—Responding to the Story | Time: |

Propose this scenario: Pretend that you are the lizard in the story. When you return to your home you find tracks going into it. What do you do? Write the story your way. Illustrate the story if time allows. Share the stories if time permits. (Students will need writing and drawing paper for this activity.)

Math—Ant Fact Families | Time: |

• Students cut out the ant manipulatives.

• Give a number, for example, 15. Students arrange their ants into two groups to make 15. Students write a number sentence. Continue to show all the possible combinations. Then develop a number family for a different number.

Science—It's an Insect! | Time: |

• Use the transparency to discuss the attributes of an insect. On the chalkboard, list the attributes that insects have in common (three body parts, six legs, and antennae).

• Have students look at the drawing of the ant and use the insect attribute list they have developed to determine whether the ant is an insect.

Music and Fun—"There's an Ant on the Rug" song and puppet | Time: |

• Sing (to the tune of "There's a Spider on the Floor") or chant the poem.

• Note the rhyme pattern and make up new verses.

> There's an ant on my cheek, on my cheek.
>
> There's an ant on my cheek, on my cheek.
>
> It's playing hide and seek, the ant on my cheek!
>
> There's an ant on my cheek, on my cheek.

• Students might illustrate new verses.

• Make ant puppets attached to craft sticks. Use the puppets to act out each of the verses as you sing the song again.

How to Plan Your School Year • EMC 779

An Ant's Voice

An East African Tale

Once upon a time an ant went to find a new house. He crawled into a lizard's home when the lizard was away. He made himself at home. When the lizard came back, it saw new tracks going into its cave. The lizard called, "Who's in my house?"

The ant yelled out in a loud voice, "It is I! I am so strong I trample elephants as I pass. Who dares to ask?" The tiny ant's voice boomed through the cave.

The lizard ran away from its home, crying, "What can I do? I cannot fight a creature who tramples elephants. How will I get my house back?"

Soon the lizard met a warthog. It asked the warthog for help. When they reached the mouth of the cave, the warthog barked loudly, "Who is in the house of my friend the lizard?"

The ant answered in a loud voice. "It is I! I am so strong I trample elephants as I pass. Who dares to ask?"

The warthog backed away from the cave. "I am sorry. I can do nothing," it said, and quickly left.

Then the lizard stopped a tiger that was passing by. The tiger told the lizard not to worry. The tiger moved to the mouth of the cave. It showed its claws and growled, "Who is in the house of my friend the lizard?"

The ant shouted back, "It is I! I am so powerful I trample elephants as I pass. Who dares to ask?"

The tiger jumped back. "The creature tramples elephants! What will it do to me? I cannot help you, friend."

The lizard was about to give up hope. Then it saw a little frog passing by. The lizard stopped the frog and asked for help. The frog went to the mouth of the cave. It asked who was inside. The ant gave the same answer, "It is I! I am so powerful I trample elephants as I pass. Who dares to ask?"

The frog took one hop into the cave and croaked back, "I, who have come at last, I dare to ask. I am the most powerful of all. I am the one who tramples those who trample elephants!"

When the ant heard this, he shook. He saw the big shadow at the mouth of the cave. He thought, "Look at the awful thing that has come to get me. I have had my fun. I have stayed in the cave long enough." The ant crept out of the cave.

The lizard and the other animals nearby pounced on the ant. "You!" the animals cried. "You are only an ant! The cave's echo made your voice big and loud. We thought you were big and mean."

The ant stared at the frog. "And you, Frog, your shadow made me think you were huge."

The animals laughed at themselves. The ant scurried away.

What Did It Say?

1. What animal lived in the cave?

_____

2. What animal made itself at home in the cave?

_____

3. How did the animal answer the other animals' questions?

_____

_____

4. What animal was able to make the cave visitor leave?

_____

5. Why was the ant's voice so loud?

_____

_____

6. Why was the frog's shadow so big?

_____

_____

_____

_____

How to Plan Your School Year • EMC 779

Name: _____

What Did It Say?

Complete the sentences using the words in the Word Box.

1. A rhinoceros is a _____ animal.

2. An elephant _____ the grass when it runs.

3. The ant's voice _____ through the cave.

4. The little mouse _____ along.

5. The tiger _____ on its dinner.

tramples	scurried	echoed
pounced	powerful	

■ ■ ■ Opposites ■ ■ ■

Color in the circles to show the opposites.

big	little	huge	rig
weak	meek	beak	strong
loud	crowd	quiet	noisy
stop	halt	go	crop
ask	answer	question	task
laugh	half	giggle	cry

How to Plan Your School Year • EMC 779

There's an Ant on the Rug

There's an ant on the rug, on the rug.
There's an ant on the rug, on the rug.
What a tiny bug, little ant on the rug.
There's an ant on the rug, on the rug.

There's an ant on my ear, on my ear.
There's an ant on my ear, on my ear.
I have nothing to fear from the ant on my ear.
There's an ant on my ear, on my ear.

There's an ant on my toe, on my toe.
There's an ant on my toe, on my toe.
Where will it go, that ant on my toe?
There's an ant on my toe, on my toe.

There's an ant on my nose, on my nose.
There's an ant on my nose, on my nose.
What do you suppose? An ant on my nose!
There's an ant on my nose, on my nose.

There's an ant on my knee, on my knee.
There's an ant on my knee, on my knee.
It's climbing up on me. An ant on my knee!
There's an ant on my knee, on my knee.

There's an ant in my hair, in my hair.
There's an ant in my hair, in my hair.
I am very aware there's an ant in my hair.
There's an ant in my hair, in my hair.

There's an ant on my arm, on my arm.
There's an ant on my arm, on my arm.
It won't do any harm, the ant on my arm.
There's an ant on my arm, on my arm.

There's an ant in a jar, in a jar.
There's an ant in a jar, in a jar.
It traveled near and far, but now it's in a jar.
There's an ant in a jar, in a jar.

Cut out and glue to a craft stick to use as a puppet.

How to Plan Your School Year • EMC 779

Ant Fact Families

How to Plan Your School Year • EMC 779

It's an Insect!

These creatures are insects:

 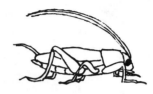

These creatures are not insects:

 Is the ant an insect? _____
Tell why or why not.

_____

_____

_____

_____

_____

How to Plan Your School Year • EMC 779

General Directions

Pages 296–303 contain substitute plans for an intermediate classroom based on the theme "Breaking Records."

- Reproduce the lesson plan on page 296. Indicate the time period when each activity should be conducted.
- Reproduce the student pages detailed below.
- File the plans in your sub folder. In an emergency, your sub plans will be ready.
- In the event that further activities may be needed, leave additional resources such as other tall tales or biographies of real record breakers such as Jesse Owens, along with follow-up suggestions.

Plan Specifics

Reading

Jesse O
Reproduce the story on pages 297 and 298, the comprehension questions on page 299, and the vocabulary sheet on page 300.

Writing

- Reproduce the instruction page on page 301.
- Provide writing paper.

Math

- Make a transparency of the chart on page 302.
- Reproduce page 302 for each student.

Science

- Reproduce the spinner pattern on page 303.
- Provide paper clips.

Dear Substitute,

Here are lesson plans to use in my absence. The theme for these fun activities is **Breaking Records**. All the student activity pages have been reproduced and are included in this folder.
Thank you.

Reading—*Jesse O* | Time: |

- Read this tall tale.

- Complete the comprehension and vocabulary worksheets.

Writing—Tall Tales | Time: |

- Discuss the attributes of tall tales.

- Read the Writing Your Own Tall Tale information sheet.

- Write an original tall tale.

Math—Reading a Chart | Time: |

- Discuss the chart provided on the transparency. Ask several questions to make sure students can read the chart.

   Who held the record for the 400-meter run in 1998?

   Why are there two times and two record holders for each event?

- Have students answer the questions on their copy of the page.

Science—Make It Faster | Time: |

- This hands-on science activity is easily done in the classroom or on the playground.

- Have each student make a spinner.

- Develop ways in which the fall of the spinner might be timed—clock or watches with second hands, counting, tapping foot, singing a song, clapping a rhythm, etc.

- Drop the spinners and watch them spin.

- Have students modify the spinners to make them spin slower or faster.

- Race for the class record.

How to Plan Your School Year • EMC 779

Jesse O

Jesse O grew up in Alabama, where his parents were sharecroppers. They planted and harvested crops on someone else's land for a share of the crop's profit. When he was a little boy, Jesse O was so sickly and thin that when he turned sideways he disappeared. Jesse ran through the fields and got thinner and thinner. Soon he was thinner than the tiny twigs on the willow tree that grew by the shack where he lived.

Jesse ran farther and farther each day. When he was nine, Jesse ran all the way to Ohio, pulling his family to a better life. It was there that he learned that "track" was more than stalking an animal.

Jesse was no longer a skinny kid who ran with the wind. He was like a powerful racing car. He ran so hard that the soles melted off his shoes. He jumped so high that the principal of his junior high school called him to get balls thrown onto the roof. Jesse ran and jumped himself into a legend.

You see, Jesse started running in track-and-field meets. He ran the 100-yard dash so quickly that the timers thought their watches were broken. Jesse piled up the victories. The pile of medals he won was so tall that even he couldn't jump over it. He broke so many records that the record keeper made a rubber stamp that said "Jesse O." That way, whenever Jesse set a new record, he could just stamp the name in the record book.

Jesse was so fast that his coaches had trouble locating him in the stadium. They finally put a spotter at each of his events. The spotter's job was to raise a banner when Jesse started competing. Sometimes Jesse finished one event and started another before the spotter at the first event could raise the banner!

297

Jesse O grew faster and stronger with every race he ran. Soon he was running 'round the world. He could finish a race in Berlin and make the start of the long jump in Chicago. As he ran, drops of sweat fell to the ground causing flash floods in Oklahoma. Sparks from his shoes started brush fires in Africa. TV weathermen gave Jesse O weather alerts so that those in his path could be prepared.

Jesse leaped across the Atlantic, and ocean liners were pulled into his wake. He broke every record there was to break. He ran every race there was to run. He even ran some races that weren't races yet.

Jesse O blazed a trail that runners today still follow. He ran so fast and so hard that he became a part of every track he ran on. If you are ever running and the wind is whistling by your ears, you may feel Jesse's hand in your own pulling you forward. His gentle voice may whisper words of encouragement. Jesse O ran his last race a long time ago. But he is still at every track. His skin is still as black as the cinders. His eyes are still as bright as the stars. His heart is still as big as the world he ran through many years ago.

How to Plan Your School Year • EMC 779

Name: _____

Questions about Jesse O

1. What does **track and field** mean as it is used in this tall tale?

_____

_____

2. How did the man in charge of records keep up with Jesse O?

_____

_____

3. How did Jesse's coaches find him in the stadium?

_____

_____

4. What potential dangers did Jesse pose for people in his path?

_____

_____

5. What were some of Jesse's accomplishments?

_____

_____

_____

6. Think of a nickname you might give Jesse O. Write it here.

_____

How to Plan Your School Year • EMC 779

Name: _____

Homonyms

Homonyms are words that sound the same but are spelled differently.

sole—soul   brake—break   raise—rays

Use the correct word in each sentence. Then illustrate the sentence with a cartoon drawing.

The _____ of his
shoe had a hole in it.

The _____ of the
sun melted the ice cream.

He will _____ the
record for longest beard.

_____ the flag
above your head.

Pick another homonym pair. _____

On the back of the page, write a sentence and draw a picture for each word in the pair.

How to Plan Your School Year • EMC 779

Writing Your Own Tall Tale

Many tall tales were inspired by real people. The tale of Jesse O is based on the life of Jesse Owens, a legend in American track and field. Here is a factual account of Jesse Owens' life.

Jesse Owens was the son of Alabama sharecroppers. As a child he was skinny and often sick. When he was nine, his family moved to Ohio to find a better life. It was there, when he was in junior high school, Jesse met his mentor. Charles Riley was a gym teacher and coach of the track team. Coach Riley taught Jesse to run and jump. Jesse worked hard. He set his first track-and-field record in that same year. He ran the 100-yard dash in ten seconds flat. He went on to set many records in high school and college. At the 1936 Olympics in Berlin, Jesse won four gold medals as he set new world records in three events. One of the greatest track-and-field athletes of the United States, Jesse Owens began life as a poor, sickly boy and became a world hero.

1. List some of the things that happened in the tall tale about Jesse O that are based on actual events in Jesse Owens' life.

_____   _____   _____

_____   _____   _____

2. Name a famous sports figure. _____

List some of his or her accomplishments.

_____   _____

_____   _____

How to Plan Your School Year • EMC 779

Interpreting Records

Use this chart to answer the questions below.

Track-and-Field Records—October 1998

Event	Record	Holder	Country
100 meters	9.84 seconds	Donovan Bailey	Canada
	10.49 seconds	Florence Griffith Joyner	U.S.
200 meters	19.32 seconds	Michael Johnson	U.S.
	21.34 seconds	Florence Griffith Joyner	U.S.
400 meters	43.29 seconds	Harry Reynolds	U.S.
	47.60 seconds	Marita Koch	E. Germany
800 meters	1 minute, 41.11 seconds	Wilson Kipketer	Denmark
	1 minute, 53.28 seconds	Jarmila Kratochvilova	Czechoslovakia
1000 meters	2 minutes, 12.18 seconds	Sebastian Coe	Great Britain
	2 minutes, 26.98 seconds	Svetlana Masterkova	Russia

1. How much faster is the man's record than the woman's record in each category?

2. If Donovan Bailey could run 200 meters at the same speed per hundred meters, would his time be faster than Michael Johnson's time?

3. What is the average difference between the men's and the women's records?

4. How many of the record holders are from the U.S.? Express that number as a fraction and a percent.

How to Plan Your School Year • EMC 779

Making It Faster

Cut, color, and fold the spinner.

Put a paper clip on the end of the spinner to hold the folds in place.

Drop the spinner.

Time the spinner flight.

Now change the spinner in one way. Here are three possible changes:

- Fold the flaps up on the ends.
- Fold both flaps in one direction.
- Add a paper clip.

Does it go faster or slower?

Record each change and tell whether it was faster or slower than the original spinner.

Change	Result

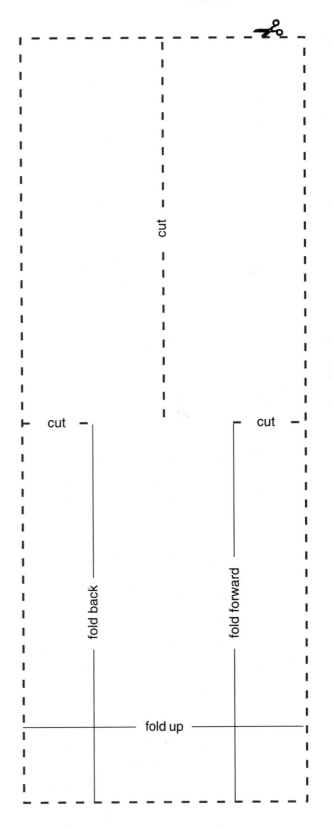

Last Thoughts

When you are a teacher you are always in the right place at the right time. There is no wrong time for learning. It may be the wrong time for what the teacher had planned to teach, but just as certainly it will be the perfect time to teach something else. Teachers learn to grasp the moment. Any time a student is there before you, the possibility is present, the moment is yours.

Betty B. Anderson

Education is not a product: mark, diploma, job, money—in that order; it is a process, a never-ending one.

Bel Kaufman

The mediocre teacher tells. The good teacher explains. The superior teacher demonstrates. The great teacher inspires.

William Arthur Ward

The classroom and teacher occupy the most important part, the most important position of the human fabric.... In the schoolhouse we have the heart of the whole society.

Henry Golden

How to Plan Your School Year • EMC 779